THE BOOK OF THE
POPPY

THE BOOK OF THE
POPPY

CHRIS McNAB

FOREWORD BY VICE ADMIRAL PETER WILKINSON, CB CVO,
NATIONAL PRESIDENT, THE ROYAL BRITISH LEGION

First published 2014

The History Press
The Mill, Brimscombe Port
Stroud, Gloucestershire, GL5 2QG
www.thehistorypress.co.uk

British Library Cataloguing in Publication Data.
A catalogue record for this book is available from the British Library.

ISBN 978 0 7509 6049 6

Typesetting and origination by The History Press

CONTENTS

Vice Admiral Peter Wilkinson, CB CVO
National President, The Royal British Legion

FOREWORD

In Flanders fields the poppies blow
Between the crosses, row on row …

John McCrae

POPPIES, WHICH GROW abundantly in northern France and which were commented upon by many of the soldiers fighting there, were suggested as a symbol of Remembrance to mark the enormous human cost of the First World War following the publication of John McCrae's poem 'In Flanders Fields'. They were adopted by the American Legion in 1920 and a year later by the newly formed British Legion, as the emblem for its first fundraising campaign, now known everywhere as the Poppy Appeal.

The 4th of August 2014 marks the 100th anniversary of the day Britain entered the First World War – one of the costliest conflicts in history. This book will provide you with an understanding of the history of the poppy and its significance as a unique and enduring symbol that represents the Legion's vital work for the Armed Forces community.

Nearly a century on, that work is more important than ever. The problems faced by serving personnel, veterans and their dependents today are very similar to those that faced soldiers returning from the First World War; whether living with bereavement or disability, finding employment, or coping with financial stress. The Legion is currently spending £1.6 million each week to provide vital care and support to the Armed Forces community and we intend to be here for the next 100 years to ensure that the needs of all our beneficiaries continue to be met.

Thank you for purchasing *The Book of the Poppy*. It is with great pleasure, respect and gratitude that I, as National President of The Royal British Legion, invite you to join me in reflecting on what the poppy has meant to past generations and what it still means to us today.

Vice Admiral Peter Wilkinson, CB CVO
National President, The Royal British Legion

INTRODUCTION

WAR HAS UNDENIABLY shaped Britain, historically and socially. For there have been relatively few prolonged periods in British history when the nation has not been embroiled in domestic or foreign conflict. These conflicts have cost the lives of millions of soldiers and thousands of civilians, blood being spilt in every corner of the globe across the centuries. Yet this constant immersion in conflict does not seem to have stripped the nation of its humanity. Indeed, it is a somewhat warming truth that in many ways we have become more, not less, reflective on the nature of conflict and its human cost.

Every year in the United Kingdom, in October and running into November, a distinctive accessory is attached to the clothing of millions of people. This accessory is unusual in that it isn't about fashion, nor is it purely about fundraising (although this is a major part of the rationale behind its distribution). Instead, it is a very visible national act of commemoration. It is the Remembrance Poppy.

In its typical form, the Remembrance Poppy is not an item of material worth. It is basically a poppy rendered in paper and plastic, the vivid red paper petals standing out clearly and attractively atop a green plastic stem. And yet, there are few items worn with more reflection and pride. It represents a collective act of remembrance for generations of British war dead, especially the nation's military personnel. At the same time it also compels us to think about all those who have died in conflict, including Britain's former enemies, and those who continue to suffer the effects of war, whether veterans of previous conflicts or victims of present ones. In many ways, therefore, each poppy represents not just loss, but the continuing desire to care for those affected by war.

This short book is published to coincide with the centenary of the beginning of the First World War (1914–18). A hundred years ago, a shot rang out on the streets of Sarajevo, the assassin's bullet inflicting mortal wounds on the Austro-Hungarian Archduke Franz Ferdinand. Four years later, through a scarcely conceivable chain reaction of events, 20 million people lay dead and large parts of Europe, Africa and the Middle East were in ruin. The magnitude and human cost of this conflict still reverberate today, even in light of the subsequent world war between 1939 and 1945, which killed more than 50 million.

Furthermore, the end of the Second World War did not see an end to global conflict – sadly there has not been a single year since 1945 in which war has not been fought somewhere around the globe. British soldiers have continued to fight, die and endure to the present day. The Remembrance Poppy, therefore, has never been more relevant.

Chris McNab, 2014

1. NATION AT WAR

IT IS UNDENIABLE that Britain has a particularly distinguished military history and martial tradition. What is often remarkable about this history is that is has generally been achieved with a comparatively small armed forces. Looking back to the medieval age, the martial burden of the nation was taken by a militia – a non-professional citizen army. Various royal statutes placed obligations for male citizens to serve in the militia at times of crisis, led by the noble knights who owed feudal service to the king or queen. There were very few of what we would know as 'standing forces' (full-time professional soldiers) – isolated examples include the Yeoman of the Guard, essentially a professional royal bodyguard force created by Henry VII in 1485 at the Battle of Bosworth Field. It should also be noted that the medieval monarchs drew heavily upon foreign mercenaries to patch the gaps in military capability – Britain's armies have frequently been international bodies.

The soldiers of the medieval militias were kept busy through an endless sequence of destructive wars, from bitter civil conflicts such as the War of the Roses (1455–1487) to distant expeditionary adventures like the Crusades in the Middle East. Hundreds of thousands of British citizens served and died for causes truly remote from their daily lives and concerns, although the ferocity with which they fought gave the British renown as a warrior race.

The nature of Britain's armed forces changed considerably during the sixteenth and seventeenth centuries, not least in terms of maritime power. By the sixteenth century, the nation had already established a 'Navy Royal', a force of State-owned warships and naval facilities. The size and power of the force waxed and waned, the British fleet often supplemented by private vessels to fight its wars. Crises were averted, such as the repulsion of the Spanish Armada in 1588 (as much by virtue of the resistant British weather as its navy), but as an island nation Britain needed a more formidable fleet. This ambition was realised in the seventeenth century, as the Navy Royal expanded under both Charles I (r. 1625–49) and II (r. 1660–85) and the rule of Oliver Cromwell/the Commonwealth that separated the kings' rule. Through major programmes of shipbuilding, fuelled by conflicts such as the Third Anglo-Dutch War (1672–74) and the War of the

Grand Alliance (1688–97), Britain acquired a 'Royal Navy' and became the most powerful naval force on the planet for the next 200 years.

The army was also changing. Queen Elizabeth's long-running war against the Spanish in the Netherlands from 1595 demanded huge amounts of manpower. Although still using the militia system, Elizabeth oversaw a degree of professionalisation of the army, particularly in terms of command and administration, but it still didn't give Britain a stable force. Ironically, it took revolution to transform Britain's land forces. Following the overthrow and execution of Charles I, Oliver Cromwell's 'New Model Army' became Britain's first professional standing army. It was well-trained, liable for service in any destination (previously many militias had just been bound to service in a single local area) and had a professional officer class. Although the Commonwealth collapsed in 1660, with the restoration of Charles II, the new monarch saw the clear value of a standing army, and began to build up his own. This army swelled rapidly – it reached about 40,000 men strong under James II (1685–88) – and was structured around a regimental system that still exists today. This system, which first emerged in the sixteenth century, created formations of soldiers with a fierce sense of local identity and geographical connection. (The practice of creating county, as opposed to numbered, regiments was actually implemented by Richard Haldane, the British Secretary of State for War between 1905 and 1912.)

By the time Britain had a standing army, the nature of warfare had changed almost beyond recognition compared to the medieval period. Gunpowder was now a force on the battlefield. Crude cannon and 'hand-gonnes' (effectively the first small-arms) had been introduced into Europe in the fourteenth century. As the weapons developed in power and dependability, they had a fundamental impact on the social and political fabric of the nation. The castle, the traditional seat of noble power, could now be cracked open by gunpowder artillery (although this process still required some thunderous persistence) and humble infantry armed with musket firearms could kill the most esteemed knight, despite having just days training as opposed to the years required to create a professional archer. By the seventeenth century, the muskets were using flintlock mechanisms that gave faster and consistent volley fire, while the artillery was more mobile and devastating, wheeled into position on the battlefield to deliver terrible hails of solid ball and grape shot. Although much killing was still done at close quarters with bayonet and blade, now the bulk of the slaughter was performed at a distance by gunpowder weaponry.

Britain's professional military units were certainly kept busy during the eighteenth and nineteenth centuries. Following the 1707 Act of Union between England and Scotland, the land forces were a truly 'British Army', and under leaders such as Marlborough and Wellington it became (and remains) a globally respected force. It was ever more international in its involvements, participating in coalition conflicts such as the War of the Spanish Succession (1701–1714), the Seven Years' War (1754–63) and the Napoleonic Wars (1803–15). At the same time, the British established the largest empire the world had ever seen, so thousands of men found themselves deployed to truly remote corners of the world, effectively as imperial police forces.

Britain, however, still relied heavily on private soldiers and militias to fulfil its military obligations. For many years India was governed with the assistance of the private armies of the East India Company (EIC), and even during the French Revolutionary and Napoleonic Wars the British forces were heavily reliant upon various volunteer, yeomanry (volunteer cavalry) and militia defence forces. Only in the early twentieth century was the situation given a greater degree of order through Haldane's Territorial and Reserve Forces Act of 1907, which organised non-State units into the Territorial Force. The Territorial Force eventually became what we know today as the Territorial Army, and this critical reserve force has served with distinction in most major British conflicts from the First World War to the present day.

Britain entered the twentieth century with a historically battle-proven army, one that really did 'punch above its weight' on the world stage. It was disciplined, professional and experienced, although there were cracks in the veneer. The Crimean War (1853–56), Anglo-Zulu War (1879) and Boer Wars (1880–81, 1899–1902) had shown that while the British could still win wars, they could also suffer disastrous localised defeats if they underestimated their enemies, were led badly or miscalculated their logistical requirements. In Afghanistan in 1842, the British suffered a catastrophe when Afghan tribesmen massacred 4,500 soldiers and 12,000 camp followers, as the vast column attempted to make its escape from Kabul to Jalalabad. At the Battle of Isandlwana in South Africa on 22 January 1879, a Zulu army of 20,000 warriors destroyed an entire British force – 1,300 British soldiers died, despite having modern rifles and artillery pieces at their disposal. During the Boer War, on 23–24 January 1900, a force of Boer warriors trapped hundreds of British troops atop Spion Kop, a hill 24 miles (38km) west-south-west of Ladysmith. Over the course of a horrifying day, 243 soldiers were killed and 1,250 wounded, the hapless British trying to claw their way into solid rock to escape the merciless rifle fire. Such battles, although long distant from our present age, and fought for causes largely alien to our modern politics, still deserve to be remembered for the young men who lost their lives, on days too awful to imagine.

MAJOR BATTLES IN BRITISH HISTORY, 1066–1900

Battle	Date	Present-Day Location
Hastings	14 October 1066	Near Hastings, East Sussex
Agincourt	25 October 1415	Near Azincourt, northern France
Spanish Armada	July–September 1588	The seas around British Isles and Ireland
Blenheim	13 August 1704	Blenheim, Bavaria
Culloden	16 April 1746	Drumossie Moor, north-east of Inverness, Scotland
Quebec/ Plains of Abraham	13 September 1759	Plains of Abraham, outside Quebec, Canada
Lexington	19 April 1775	Lexington, Massachusetts, USA
Salamanca	22 July 1812	Arapiles, Salamanca, Spain
Waterloo	18 June 1815	Waterloo, Belgium
Aliwal	28 January 1846	Aliwal, Punjab, India
Balaklava	25 October 1854	Balaklava, Crimean Peninsula, Ukraine
Rorke's Drift	22–23 January 1879	On Buffalo River between Natal and the Zulu kingdom, South Africa

War
Norman Conquest of England (1066–72)
Hundred Years' War (1337–1453)
Anglo-Spanish War (1585–1604)
War of the Spanish Succession (1701–14)
Jacobite Rebellion of 1745
Seven Years' War (1754–63)
American War of Independence (1775–83)
Peninsular War (1807–14)
Napoleonic Wars (1803–15)
First Anglo-Sikh War (1845–46)
Crimean War (1853–56)
Anglo-Zulu War (1879)

THE 'GREAT WAR'

As this book is published, the world is preparing to commemorate the 100th anniversary of the beginning of the First World War. Despite its increasing historical distance, the war has a special resonance in the collective memory. Why is this so? Britain, as we have seen, has a martial tradition stretching back to ancient times, and has fought numerous consuming conflicts on foreign and domestic soils. Yet our reflections upon, say, British participation in the Seven Years' War or even the Napoleonic Wars are now far more to do with historical interest than national remembrance. The obvious reason for our ongoing connection with the First World War is its proximity. A hundred years is a long time, but there is still a generation of people alive whose parents and grandparents fought in the 'Great War'. The First World War was also the first recognisably 'modern' conflict, a clash wrought across the full spectrum of environments – air, land and sea – and with the same fundamental types of weaponry that dominate conflict today. There is also a political factor – debates over whether the First World War was a 'justified' conflict continue to rage, especially as the political repercussions and imperial engineering of the war are still felt around the globe today, particularly in the Middle East and the Balkans. Yet above all these reasons, and the true focus of the centennial commemorations, is the daunting human cost of the war, not only for the British, but also for all those nations who fought.

We start with some basic statistics to gain perspective. During the First World War, the United Kingdom had a population of just over 46 million people. Of this number, a total of 5.7 million men served in the armed forces, and within this figure around 700,000 were killed. Add to that grim total an estimated 1.6 million wounded, and some 2.3 million men – nearly half of all those who served in the war – became casualties. Yet this is not including the men and women of the British colonies and dominions (primarily Australia, New Zealand, Canada, South Africa and India), without whom Britain would have been unable to sustain many campaigns. If we add their contribution, the total figure for dead, missing and wounded amongst 'British' troops climbs to nearly 3 million.

These figures are stunning enough, but they represent the fallen of just a few of the combatant countries. Looking on the Entente side, France suffered a generational disaster in the form of nearly 1.4 million war dead, plus 4.3 million wounded. Russia's losses, to our best estimate, were

1.8 million dead and nearly 5 million wounded. It also experienced some 2 million civilian dead. (The civilian death tolls for Britain and France were 1,386 and 40,000 respectively.) Italy took 1.4 million casualties, of whom 462,000 were fatalities.

Figures for the Central Powers are just as dizzying and depressing. Germany lost at least 2 million of its soldiers in fighting on two fronts, plus 5.7 million military wounded and 700,000 civilian deaths. Austria-Hungary suffered nearly 3 million dead and wounded; 478,000 POWs also died in captivity. Turkey's casualty lists are grossly skewed towards civilian deaths – around 2 million, mainly Armenians caught by the genocide unleashed upon them from c. 1915, but also took a million military dead and wounded. When such figures and the rolls of honour of all other combatant nations are added together, the First World War cost the lives of at least 16 million people, with another 20 million wounded.

Few engagements represent the catastrophe of the First World War better than the Battle of the Somme, the British offensive fought between 1 July and 13 November 1916. On the first day of the attack alone, the British suffered 60,000 casualties, including 19,240 dead, despite the confidence that a week-long, 1.6-million-shell bombardment of the German lines would have rendered all the defenders either dead, wounded or insensible. The British soldiers, stretched along a 14-mile (23km) front, went 'over the top' under fine weather at 7.30 a.m., many of them advancing at a walking pace in expectation of limited resistance. (Moving at a steady uniform pace also allowed units and individuals to maintain effective communication links, rather than become strung out over the battlefield.) Instead, they walked into blistering hails of machine-gun fire and German artillery. Entire battalions of young men were hewn to pieces in minutes, their bodies lying out in blasted fields and amongst contorted wraps of barbed wire. Almost no significant territorial gains were made that day, and in many cases the units ended up back at their start lines, their ranks thinned down considerably compared to when they set out a few hours previously.

FIRST WORLD WAR CASUALTIES
(DEAD, WOUNDED AND MISSING)

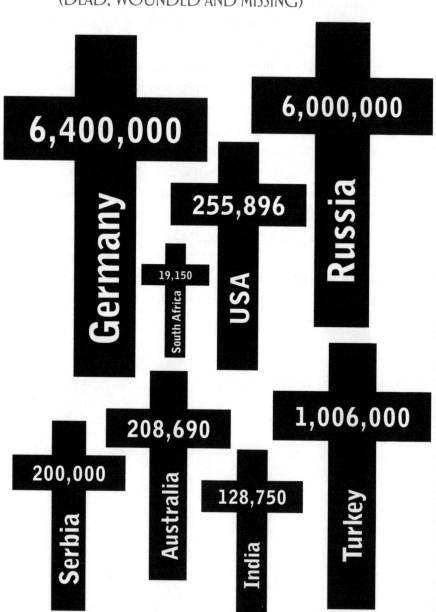

6,400,000 Germany

6,000,000 Russia

255,896 USA

19,150 South Africa

208,690 Australia

200,000 Serbia

128,750 India

1,006,000 Turkey

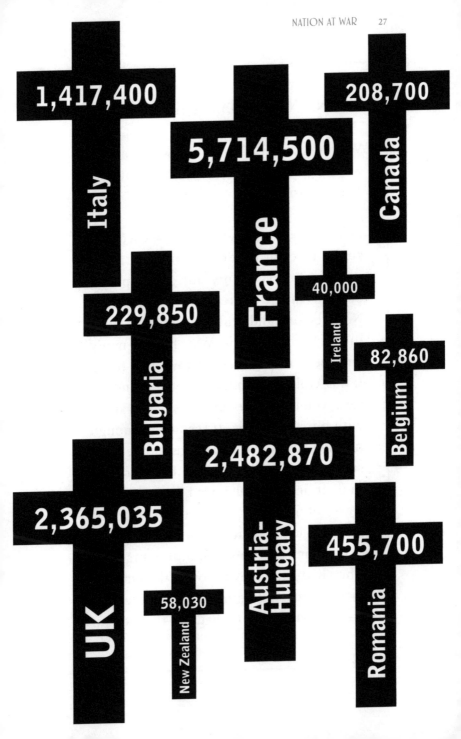

FRONTLINE VOICES: BATTLE OF THE SOMME

War reporter Philip Gibbs wrote about what he saw on the first day of the Somme, 1 July 1916:

Before dawn there was a great silence. We spoke to each other in whispers, if we spoke. Then suddenly our guns opened out in a barrage of fire of colossal intensity. Never before, and I think never since, even in the Second World War, had so many guns been massed behind any battle front. It was a rolling thunder of shell fire, and the earth vomited flame, and the sky was alight with bursting shells. It seemed as though nothing could live, not an ant, under that stupendous artillery storm. But Germans in their deep dugouts lived, and when our waves of men went over they were met by deadly machine-gun and mortar fire.

Our men got nowhere on the first day. They had been mown down like grass by German machine-gunners who, after our barrage had lifted, rushed out to meet our

men in the open. Many
of the best battalions
were almost annihilated,
and our casualties were
terrible.

A German doctor taken
prisoner near La Boiselle stayed
behind to look after our wounded
in a dugout instead of going down to
safety. I met him coming back across
the battlefield next morning. One of
our men was carrying his bag and
I had a talk with him. He was a tall,
heavy man with a black beard, and
he spoke good English. 'This war!'
he said. 'We go on killing each other
to no purpose. It is a war against
religion and against civilisation and
I see no end to it.'

The poignancy of this single day was heightened by a feature of British Army recruiting practice in the early years of the First World War. At the start of the conflict in 1914, the total manpower available to the British Expeditionary Force (BEF) was just 250,000 regular troops. This was nowhere near enough to face the German onslaught in Western Europe, thus Lord Kitchener, the Secretary of State for War, on 6 August began an impassioned appeal for men to join the ranks of the military as volunteers. Hundreds of thousands of men signed up in a matter of days, causing chaos at recruiting stations and recruit training depots. The men were encouraged to join up not only by the patriotism that fuelled the early weeks of the conflict, but also in many cases by the simple desire to enlist with their friends and colleagues, often with the added bonus of escaping a grinding industrial existence in Britain. An extremely localised form of recruiting produced what were known as the 'Pals Battalions', units of men connected through living on the same street, working in the same company, or belonging to the same guild or society. Aside from their official battalion designations, these battalions had evocative titles such as the 'Hull Commercials', 'The Grimsby Chums', 'Glasgow Tramways Battalion' and 'Footballers Battalion'. Some 300 Pals Battalions were formed in 1914–15.

Looking back, the romanticism and comradeship of the Pals Battalions masked an obvious truth – if a battalion was decimated in battle, the losses would have a disproportionate effect on the home community from which the battalion was formed. Such was proved in graphic fashion at the Battle of the Somme. In the space of that single, terrible opening day, entire battalions were virtually destroyed. The Leeds Battalion lost some 700 of its 900 men, and the famous Accrington Pals – more fully known as 11th (Service) Battalion (Accrington) East Lancashire Regiment – suffered 584 dead, wounded and missing of the 750 men who had joined the attack.

The Battle of the Somme would rumble on for months to come, wavering in its intensity and the levels of human destruction. By the time it ran out of steam in November 1914, for advances of no more than 5 miles (8km), the British and French troops had taken 623,000 casualties. The Germans had also lost half a million men on the Somme – this was no one-sided battle.

As appalling as the Somme was, it sits comfortably alongside other epic battles of the war, some with even more excessive casualty lists. Also in 1916, the vast clash of arms between the Germans and French at Verdun in north-eastern France resulted in nearly one million dead and wounded between 21 February and 20 December. The battle was actually little more than a colossal exercise in attrition, the outcome of German efforts to 'bleed to death' the French Army. The British battle known as Third Ypres – more popularly called the Battle of Passchendaele after one of its key landmarks – inflicted 310,000 casualties on the BEF, and 250,000 on the German forces. Not only was this battle a horrifying trial by fire for the men involved, but the landscape itself became an enemy. Heavy rainfall, plus the high water table in the clay-heavy soil of Flanders, meant that for much of the battle men fought through an endless, ripped landscape of vacuous mud, in which both men and horses could and did drown if they fell from their duckboard walkways. In 1918, the German Michael Offensive added another 1.5 million casualties between 21 March and 18 July.

And lest we forget, the war on the Eastern Front between Germany and Russia was nothing short of apocalyptic. The Russian Brusilov Offensive, a vast Russian onslaught against German forces in the Ukraine, cost the lives or health of around 2.5 million men in the space of four-and-a-half months of fighting in June–September 1916.

Listing the casualties of battle in the First World War can eventually have a numbing effect, the statistics disconnected from the realities on the ground and the trauma suffered by those left to grieve. But the fact was that the world of warfare had changed. One hundred years previously, the armies met in battle armed with muzzle-loading flintlock muskets, capable of firing just two or three rounds a minute even in the hands of a skilled rifleman. Heavy firepower was delivered by smoothbore cannon, firing solid lumps of shot over ranges of several hundred yards. The men would frequently close up, deciding the battle with bayonets and swords.

By the time the First World War began in 1914, military traditionalism still lingered on in ideas of the nobility of the frontal assault or the grandeur of a cavalry charge. But the tools of war had changed beyond recognition. Now every infantryman had a breech-loading bolt-action rifle capable of firing fifteen rounds a minute, killing out to ranges of well over a mile. More significantly, machine guns were an integrated part of companies, battalions and divisions. A single German MG08 or British Vickers gun could send out streams of lead at around 450rpm. With such tools, the process of killing became virtually industrial – all that was required was to keep the gun fed with ammunition and the barrel cool (or changed when required) to deliver constant streams of death into the ranks of the enemy in no-man's-land.

Then there was the artillery. Artillery was now rifled and breech-loaded, meaning that it was

TOTAL MANPOWER MOBILISED
IN THE FIRST WORLD WAR

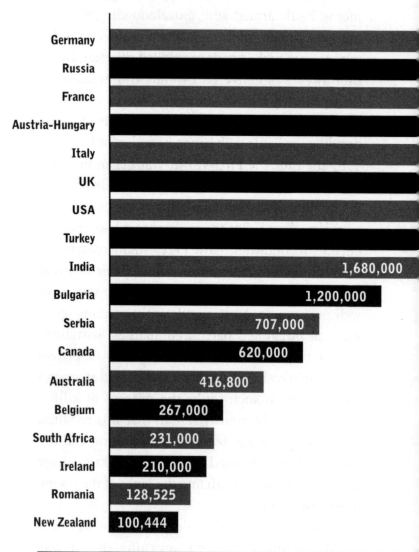

Germany	
Russia	
France	
Austria-Hungary	
Italy	
UK	
USA	
Turkey	
India	1,680,000
Bulgaria	1,200,000
Serbia	707,000
Canada	620,000
Australia	416,800
Belgium	267,000
South Africa	231,000
Ireland	210,000
Romania	128,525
New Zealand	100,444

13,400,000

12,000,000

8,660,000

7,800,000

5,903,000

4,355,000

2,600,000

accurate over great distances and had high rates of fire. Furthermore, the shells that the guns fired were filled with high-explosive, each round delivering enormous destructive effect at the point of impact. In total, some 70 per cent of all casualties in the First World War and the subsequent world war were caused by artillery, and in some armies up to 40 per cent of total military personnel were serving in the artillery arm.

There was also innovation in air and sea warfare. Although the Wright brothers had only made the first controlled, powered flight on 17 December 1903 (for the epic duration of 12 seconds), just over a decade later aircraft were being repurposed for combat. At first, the men of the Royal Flying Corps (RFC), formed in 1912, were mainly tasked with reconnaissance duties (aided by the progressive development of two-way radios and aerial cameras), flying biplane aircraft over the battlefield to provide intelligence on troop movements and artillery fire control. Onboard weaponry consisted of little more than a handgun or a grenade carried for personal defence. From 1915, however, new generations of aircraft were emerging, pure fighter types armed with machine guns, eventually synchronised to fire through the propeller (meaning the pilot could shoot along his direct line of sight), and larger bombers that could deliver bomb payloads of several thousand pounds well behind enemy frontlines. Although pilots gathered a glamorous image amongst the British public, their lives were actually brutal and short – the average life expectancy of a combat pilot on the Western Front between 1915 and 1917 was in the region of eleven days.

At sea, the war was dominated by the big-gun turreted warships. The pre-war international naval arms race had been transformed by the arrival of the Dreadnought class of warship. The type was established with HMS *Dreadnought*, a Royal Navy vessel commissioned on 2 December 1906. *Dreadnought* demonstrated a new vision of the capital warship: heavily armed with multiple large-calibre turreted guns (typically 15in and above), with ranges of many thousands of yards; powerful secondary armament; steam-turbine propulsion that gave speeds of more than 20 knots; armour applied to hulls and decks. Soon every nation was racing to produce larger and more potent versions of the Dreadnought, creating a world of metal monsters vying for control of the waves. In the First World War this led to the epic clash that was the Battle of Jutland (31 May–1 June 1916), which pitted the Royal Navy's Grand Fleet against Germany's High Seas Fleet in the North Sea off Denmark. (Note that the Grand Fleet included a significant number of

BRITISH SMALL-ARMS FIREPOWER THROUGH THE CENTURIES

GUN	7.62mm M134 Minigun
	5.56mm SA80/L85
	.303 Vickers Machine Gun
	.303 Short Magazine Lee-Enfield
	.577 Martini-Henry Rifle
	.75 British India Pattern Musket
	Medieval hand-gonne

Type: Muzzle-loading matchlock	Type: Muzzle-loading flintlock	Type: Breech-loading lever-action rifle
Effective range: c. 50m	Effective range: c. 100m	Effective range: c. 350m
Rate of fire (cyclic, per minute): 1–2	Rate of fire (cyclic, per minute): 3–4	Rate of fire (cyclic, per minute): 12

DATE IN SERVICE	13th–16th centuries	1797–1854	1871–88

Type:
Bolt-action, magazine-fed rifle

Effective range:
500–1,500m

Rate of fire (cyclic, per minute):
15

Type:
Belt-fed, recoil-operated machine gun

Effective range:
2,400–4,000m

Rate of fire (cyclic, per minute):
450–500

Type:
Gas-operated automatic rifle

Effective range:
400–500m

Rate of fire (cyclic, per minute):
Up to 775rpm

Type:
Electrically-powered, rotary-barrel machine gun (aerial mount)

Effective range:
1,000–1,500m

Rate of fire (cyclic, per minute):
Up to 4,000rpm

1907–1950s   **1912–68**   **1985–present**   **1990s–present**

Australian and New Zealand vessels and personnel.) In this thunderous engagement, nearly 9,000 men were killed and twenty-five major vessels were sunk, and both sides claimed victory. Although major fleet actions such as this were rare, they were a salutary reminder that naval personnel were far from immune from the horrors of war.

Another aspect of the naval war during the First World War was the German U-boat. Sailing from bases on the European coastline, the U-boat campaign against British shipping escalated to a policy of unrestricted submarine warfare. ('Unrestricted' meant that the U-boats would target and sink merchant vessels without warning, as opposed to operating by 'prize rules' where the ship was first stopped and the crew placed into lifeboats before the vessel was sunk.) The U-boat war, conducted primarily in the Atlantic, Mediterranean and Arctic waters, was a serious threat to the British war effort. Between 1914 and 1918, some 5,000 British vessels were sunk, costing the lives of 15,000 mariners.

As we have seen, the First World War was a seismic event on human, technological and political levels. It ended in November 1918, with a German capitulation. Although the war was a victory for the Entente powers over the German, Austro-Hungarian and Ottoman Empires, the celebrations would be muted. The war had slaughtered or crippled millions of young men. Those who survived and returned home often found post-war economies virtually ruined by four years of conflict, thus many veterans entered the ranks of the long-term unemployed. Worse still, the peace contained the seeds of another world war.

THE SECOND WORLD WAR

As is often the way following long periods of armed conflict, the British armed services suffered from a lack of investment and interest during the interwar period. By 1930 its regular army was little more than five divisions strong, the weakness in manpower compensated for partially by fourteen Territorial divisions. Britain also started to lag behind in terms of the technological advantages it had forged in the First World War, particularly regarding armoured vehicles. The evident rise of Nazi Germany during the 1930s did spur British rearmament, but when Britain went to war again in September 1939, there was no denying that it was woefully unprepared to face the might of Germany's new army and air force, which now ranked as the best in the world. (Britain's one saving grace in these early days of the conflict was the Royal Navy, which still wielded great power on the waves.)

Here is not the place, nor the space, to present a history of those apocalyptic years between 1939 and 1945. Suffice to say that the Second World War evolved into what was a 'total war', a conflict in which the combatants aimed to destroy the entire military, civilian and cultural infrastructure of the enemy. The fighting was also truly global. What started as a Northern European war spread through the Mediterranean, the Balkans, North Africa, into the Baltic States and the Soviet Union. Once Japan began its own campaign of conquest in late 1941, bringing the United States into the conflict (and widening the British theatre of operations considerably), the war zones reached out across the Pacific Ocean, from the northern coastline of Australia to the Aleutian Islands, and from humid jungle trails in Burma to sun-bleached atolls thousands of miles from continental Asia. One frequently overlooked aspect of the conflict is the war between Japan and China that had been waged on the Chinese mainland since 1937. By 1945, that aspect of the broader war had cost the lives of 20 million people.

It must also be remembered with solemnity that the estimated Soviet war dead numbered about 25 million. The war on the Eastern Front was conducted with a level of brutality and lack of pity rarely experienced anywhere else. The Soviet Union lost more people in the first weeks of the German invasion than Britain and the United States did in the entire war. German *Einsatzgruppen* (Special Purpose Units) also began to implement the first stages of the Holocaust in 1941 and 1942, conducting the mass executions of 1.1 million Jews in woods, forests, gardens and ravines. The Eastern Front had a voracious appetite for German manpower – more than 70 per cent of Germany's casualties were taken in this theatre, some 3 million soldiers.

Looking back to Britain, the Second World War was a turning point in the nation's political and military history. Between 1939 and 1941, it seemed touch and go whether the nation would survive at all. Hitler's army had conquered virtually the whole of Western Europe by June 1940, the BEF dispatched to France defeated and ejected from Dunkirk. Only the Channel separated German forces and free Britain, which now stood quite alone on the periphery of Europe. In the summer of 1940, Hitler pitted his Luftwaffe (air force) against the Royal Air Force (RAF), attempting to rid the island nation of its air cover in preparation for a planned invasion. The Battle of Britain, as it is now called, was an incredible victory for the British, brought at a heavy cost in both British and German aviators. (Within the category of 'British', we here must include the many foreign pilots who flew for the RAF, including those fighting in exile from their own Nazi-occupied countries, such as the Poles and the Czechs.) It rendered (alongside the undiminished power of the Royal Navy) a German invasion impossible, although by the autumn of 1940 Hitler's strategic focus was swinging to the east rather than the west. Nevertheless, truly awful days were ahead for the beleaguered British. The Luftwaffe unleashed the 'Blitz', a campaign of strategic bombing against British cities that ran until May 1941. Sporadic air attacks on the British mainland, plus a vicious V-1 and V-2 missile campaign from 1944, continued until nearly the end of the war. What this meant was that death came as much to Britain's civilians as it did to its military – more than 60,000 civilians died on the mainland during the war.

Looking at the wider context of the Second World War, what made it especially dreadful was the way that the lines between military and civilian targets at first blurred and then eventually collapsed completely. An estimated total of 60 million people died in the Second World War, triple the fatalities of the First World War, and more than half that figure were civilians. This imbalance was partly due to genocidal policies, none more notorious than Hitler's 'Final Solution' to the 'Jewish Question', in which 6 million of Europe's Jews were exterminated with an industrial ruthlessness that defies imagination. Yet also, air power had also reached a destructive ascendancy. Not only had the aircraft types diversified and increased in performance, but long-range strategic bombing could visit destruction on distant cities, raining high-explosives and incendiaries onto industrial targets and civilian housing areas alike. While Germany and Japan never quite developed the aircraft types or strategic focus for such bombing, the Allies unleashed hell upon Axis towns and cities, particularly between 1943 and 1945. The devastation of places such as Hamburg, Cologne and Dresden in Germany was little short of apocalyptic. In Hamburg, for example, an unrelenting pounding by British (at night) and American (by day) bombers between 24 and 28 July 1943 killed an estimated 30,000 people. During the raid a firestorm developed that generated 1,800°F (1,000°C) heat and 120mph (193km/h) windspeeds, immolating all those in its path. Japan also received the full force of strategic bombing in 1945, when US B-29 bombers began to make regular visitations. The Operation Meetinghouse air raid of 9–10 March 1945 on Tokyo has been classified as the single most destructive bombing raid in history – through using incendiaries against the city's predominantly paper-and-wood houses, the US Air Force destroyed 16 square miles (41km²) of city and killed more than 100,000 people. And of course, the ultimate expression of civilians as 'legitimate' targets came with the atomic bombings of Hiroshima and

SECOND WORLD WAR CASUALTIES
(DEAD, WOUNDED AND MISSING)

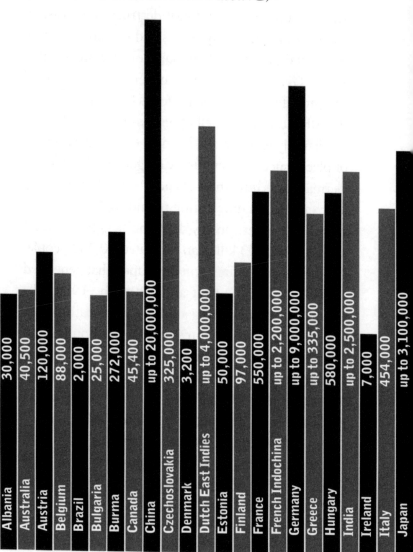

Country	Casualties
Albania	30,000
Australia	40,500
Austria	120,000
Belgium	88,000
Brazil	2,000
Bulgaria	25,000
Burma	272,000
Canada	45,400
China	up to 20,000,000
Czechoslovakia	325,000
Denmark	3,200
Dutch East Indies	up to 4,000,000
Estonia	50,000
Finland	97,000
France	550,000
French Indochina	up to 2,200,000
Germany	up to 9,000,000
Greece	up to 335,000
Hungary	580,000
India	up to 2,500,000
Ireland	7,000
Italy	454,000
Japan	up to 3,100,000

Country	Figure
Korea	up to 483,000
Latvia	230,000
Lithuania	350,000
Luxembourg	2,000
Malaya	100,000
Netherlands	301,000
New Zealand	11,900
Norway	15,000
Papua and New Guinea	15,000
Philippines	c. 1,000,000
Poland	up to 5,820,000
Portuguese Timor	up to 70,000
Romania	800,000
Ruanda–Urundi	up to 300,000
Singapore	50,000
South Africa	11,900
South Pacific Mandate	57,000
Soviet Union	up to 28,000,000
Thailand	7,600
United Kingdom	450,900
United States	418,500
Yugoslavia	1,027,000

FRONTLINE VOICES: THE BLITZ

The following is an extract from the *Manchester Guardian*, recording just one of many incidents during the Blitz:

Children sleeping in perambulators and mothers with babies in their arms were killed when a bomb exploded on a crowded shelter in an East London district during Saturday night's raids. By what is described as 'a million-to-one chance' the bomb fell directly on to a ventilator shaft measuring only about three feet by one foot. It was the only vulnerable place in a powerfully protected underground shelter accommodating over 1,000 people. The rest of the roof is well protected by three feet of brickwork, earth, and other defences, but over the ventilator shaft there were only corrugated iron sheets. The bomb fell just as scores of families were settling down in the shelter to sleep there for the night. Three or four roof-support pillars were torn down and about fourteen people were killed and some forty injured.

In one family three children were killed, but their parents escaped. Although explosions could be heard in all directions and the scene was illuminated by the glow of the East End fires, civil defence workers laboured fearlessly among the wreckage seeking the wounded, carrying them to safer places, and attending to their wounds before the ambulances arrived.

Manchester Guardian,
9 September 1940

Nagasaki on 6 and 9 August 1945 respectively. Two cities were vaporised in two instants, and the new era of nuclear warfare was inaugurated.

BRITISH BOMBER CREWS

Although British bomber crews delivered some of the most devastating raids of the war against German cities, they in turn faced the worst odds of survival of almost any branch of service. The threats they encountered included swarms of German fighters and night-fighters, dense anti-aircraft fire, enemy radar (which alerted enemy gun and fighter crews long before the bombers arrived on target), adverse weather and mechanical failure. Some 125,000 men served in Bomber Command, and 55,573 were killed, a mortality rate of 44 per cent. Bomber crewman life expectancy dropped to around six weeks in 1943–44, much less than that of an infantry officer in the trenches of the First World War.

Returning to the military campaign, Britain's armed services casualties during the conflict were significantly fewer than the First World War, although the figure of 383,000 is still chilling. During the six years of war, the armed services grew in size (via conscription), professionalism, technological might and influence. They fought in every conceivable theatre, environment and condition – the jungles of Burma, the deserts of North Africa, the icy landscapes of Norway, the mountains of Italy, the hedgerows of Normandy, the bitter Arctic and Atlantic waters and the skies above Western Europe. Armour, artillery and air power became the war-winning instruments, while on the oceans the supremacy of the battleship was replaced by the aircraft carrier, a weapon system chiefly developed by the United States and Japan. There were also new types of soldier – each side developed units (such as the British Special Air Service) of what we would now refer to as 'special forces', men tasked with the most dangerous and secretive of assignments, generally well behind enemy lines.

Given the way the Second World War engulfed the planet in destruction, it seems almost churlish to speak of winners and losers. Yet the fact remains that not only did Britain, through the efforts of its armed forces, avoid the fate of occupation that visited much of the rest of Europe, it also played a critical role in liberating territories from Nazi and imperial Japanese control. At the same time, we must recognise that these ultimate goals would have been impossible without the vast military and industrial resources of the United States and the Soviet Union. By 1945 Britain was somewhat in the shadow of these emergent superpowers, but we nevertheless owe a debt of gratitude to the generation of those years, who in many ways literally made possible the freedoms we take for granted today.

MODERN WORLD, MODERN WARS

The post-Second World War era has been a turbulent time for the Britain's armed forces. From 1945 to the present day there have been two competing demands. The first is economic pressure. The armed forces have been through numerous periods of cutbacks in both manpower and spending on resources and technology. Yet running against the grain of the cutbacks has been the fact that Britain's armed forces have rarely seen a year when they were not in action. Some of these conflicts have been major, such as the Korean War (1950–53), the Falklands War (1982), the First Gulf War (1990–91), the Iraq War (2003–2011) and the war in Afghanistan (2001–present), the latter being the longest-running continuous conflict in

British history. At the same time, British soldiers have served in numerous insurgency and peacekeeping conflicts, low-level but destructive wars that can see a soldier's role fluctuate between 'hearts-and-minds' humanitarian work and outright combat with dizzying regularity. Such actions include the Malayan Emergency (1948–60), the campaign in Aden (1964–68), long and testing service in Northern Ireland (1969–98) and operations in the war-torn Balkans in the 1990s.

The nature of warfare since 1945 could not have seen more dramatic transformations. Almost every aspect of combat technology has been revolutionised by computerisation, so that today we are no longer amazed by pilotless unmanned aerial vehicles (UAVs), precision-guided munitions (PGMs) that can hit pin-point targets after miles of flight, and military surveillance satellites that can map the battlefield in real time from hundreds of kilometres above the surface of the earth. The emphasis on technological solutions to military problems, plus a deeper political aversion to casualties amongst many nations, has thankfully resulted in a definite limitation of battlefield death tolls. For example, most British infantry divisions fighting in Normandy in 1944 would have taken more casualties in a week than the entire British losses in the Afghanistan conflict.

Yet such comparisons rather miss the point. Britain's soldiers, sailors and airmen have continued, and will continue, to make the ultimate sacrifice in war at home and aboard. For the dead and wounded, and their families, the impact is the same whether the casualties of an engagement number in the thousands or just a single individual is lost.

2. AN ACT OF REMEMBRANCE

TO TRACE THE history of the Remembrance Poppy, we have to journey back to a time and place stripped of almost all beauty and compassion. Belgian Flanders represented the northernmost point of the Western Front during the First World War, once the trenchlines had been inscribed in the earth by the end of 1914. Between 1914 and 1918, Flanders became one of the most devastated regions of the entire battlefield. The British held a salient – in effect a bulge in the frontline – that kept the city of Ypres in Allied hands and which also projected out into the German lines. Holding the salient was a nagging strategic and tactical headache for the British. The salient was overlooked by a series of German-occupied elevated ridgelines, on which they had well-sited observation posts for guiding artillery fire onto the British positions. Some military leaders argued that holding the salient was too costly, and that the British should fall back to straighten their frontline and make it more defendable. Yet the most senior levels of British command, including General Douglas Haig, Commander-in-Chief of the BEF, and Admiral Jellicoe, the First Sea Lord, argued vociferously that no more ground could be relinquished in Flanders. To do so would run the risk of the future German offensive striking through Ypres and taking valuable Channel ports (the Germans were already in possession of ports such as Ostend and Zeebrugge), which would in turn affect Allied logistics in the northern battlefront. At the same time, the Ypres salient provided a potential jumping-off point for future Allied offensives aimed at striking through the German ridgelines and swinging north to capture the German-occupied ports, which were used as bases for the predatory U-boats. For the Germans, the need to protect those ports, plus the political and strategic incentives to hang onto large portions of Belgium, meant that they had to contain the salient or even, ideally, snuff it out.

Ypres and Flanders, therefore, were to be the locations of no fewer than five major offensive battles during the war years. (Between these battles there was an ongoing and almost continuous exchange of artillery fire over the frontlines, killing and wounding men on a daily basis and reducing the once-beautiful city of Ypres to a gutted ruin.) Some of the battles were true landmarks in military history. The Second Battle of Ypres (often given in the shorthand 'Second Ypres'), was a powerful German effort to eradicate the salient, made more insidious by including the first major use of poison gas in warfare. The German forces unleashed chlorine gas in huge quantities, laying it onto the prevailing winds from 5,730 canisters emplaced near the frontline. Despite the fact that poison gas was strictly forbidden by Article 23 of the Hague Convention, from this point on it became a fixed element in the arsenals of both sides, delivered either by canister or (later and more commonly) by artillery shell. The offensive did not achieve its ultimate goal of taking Ypres, but the perimeter of the salient did shrink further, perilously close to the city.

WESTERN FRONT 1914–18

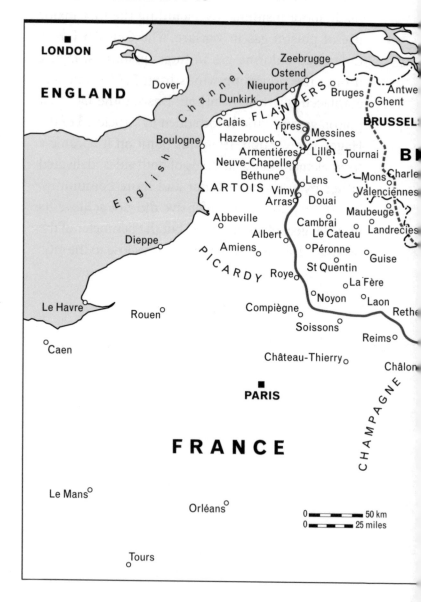

DULCE ET DECORUM EST

Bent double, like old beggars under sacks,
Knock-kneed, coughing like hags, we cursed
through sludge,
Till on the haunting flares we turned our backs
And towards our distant rest began to trudge.
Men marched asleep. Many had lost their boots
But limped on, blood-shod. All went lame;
all blind;
Drunk with fatigue; deaf even to the hoots
Of tired, outstripped Five-Nines that
dropped behind.

Gas! Gas! Quick, boys! – An ecstasy
of fumbling,
Fitting the clumsy helmets just in time;
But someone still was yelling out
and stumbling,
And flound'ring like a man in fire or lime …
Dim, through the misty panes and thick
green light,
As under a green sea, I saw him drowning.

In all my dreams, before my helpless sight,
He plunges at me, guttering, choking, drowning.

If in some smothering dreams you too
could pace
Behind the wagon that we flung him in,
And watch the white eyes writhing in his face,
His hanging face, like a devil's sick of sin;
If you could hear, at every jolt, the blood
Come gargling from the froth-corrupted lungs,
Obscene as cancer, bitter as the cud
Of vile, incurable sores on innocent tongues,
My friend, you would not tell with such high zest
To children ardent for some desperate glory,
The old Lie; *Dulce et Decorum est*
Pro patria mori.

Wilfred Owen, 1917

Another notable offensive, this time British, was 'Third Ypres', also known as the Battle of Passchendaele. Conducted between 31 July and 10 November 1917, it was the attempt to break out of the salient, take the strategic ridgelines and push through the German positions to threaten the U-boat bases further north. (The offensive also served to keep pressure on the German Army at a time when the French Army was struggling with mutiny and disarray after the failed 'Nivelle Offensive' earlier in the year.) Third Ypres was meant to be a bold and decisive offensive, but in the event it became one of the most disastrous episodes in military history. As noted in the previous chapter, the landscape during the battle became as much as a threat as the bullets and shells, and men fought through appalling physical conditions to take landmarks that were often little more than patches of rubble surrounded by oceans of mud.

GROSS TONNAGE OF BRITISH VESSELS LOST TO U-BOATS, 1914–18

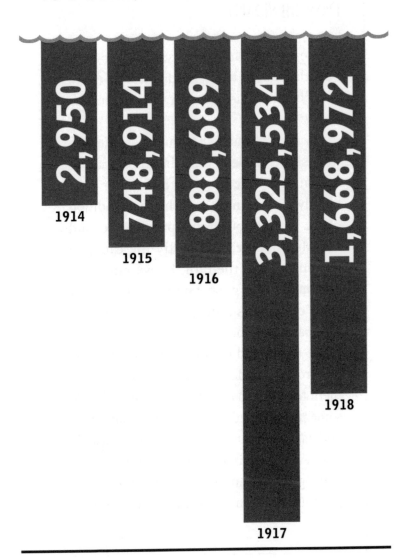

2,950 1914

748,914 1915

888,689 1916

3,325,534 1917

1,668,972 1918

FRONTLINE VOICES: THE BATTLE OF PASSCHENDAELE

The journalist Philip Gibbs, present on the Passchendaele battlefield, attempted to describe the landscape of death they faced:

Every man of ours who fought on the way to Passchendaele agreed that those battles in Flanders were the most awful, the most bloody, and the most hellish. The condition of the ground, out from Ypres and beyond the Menin Gate, was partly the cause of the misery and the filth. Heavy rains fell, and made one great bog in which every shell crater was a deep pool. There were thousands of shell craters. Our guns had made them, and German gunfire, slashing our troops, made thousands more, linking them together so that they were like lakes in some places, filled with slimy water and dead bodies. Our infantry had to advance heavily laden with their kit, and with arms and hand-grenades and entrenching tools – like pack animals – along slimy duckboards on which it was hard to keep a footing, especially at night when the battalions were moved under cover of darkness.

You live for days in the closest contact with your comrades in a contracted space. You cannot move, and are unable to think clearly. Never did I realize how difficult it can be to lead a human life. There is nameless agony in it.

Philip Gibbs,
Adventures in Journalism, 1923

The Battle of Passchendaele resonates in the imagination even today, as it presents a picture of normally picturesque Flanders transformed into a hell on earth. Yet as many soldiers noticed, in Flanders and in other regions of the blasted frontline, nature had still not given up on the land.

Papaver rhoeas is known by many other common names – corn poppy, corn rose, field poppy, red poppy and red weed. The last name on the list here is revealing, for although this member of the poppy family produces a beautiful vivid red flower, it is nonetheless classified as a weed. It grows in the most ravaged and inhospitable of land (indeed it thrives best in soil that has been disturbed), hence it managed to add a haunting dash of colour to the shell-thrashed landscape of Flanders in the late spring, summer and early autumn each year. Another of its common names is the Flanders Poppy.

To see such beautiful flowers growing across fields that were already sown with the bodies of thousands of dead men must have left an impression on the minds of all who witnessed it, the flowers delivering a curiously mixed evocation of the red blood of the fallen yet the regeneration of new life. One man who was certainly captured by the vision was the Canadian soldier Lieutenant-Colonel John Alexander McCrae.

'IN FLANDERS FIELDS'

McCrae was born on 30 November 1872, and went on to combine strong careers in both medicine and soldiering. He served as an artilleryman during the Boer War, after which he worked as a physician and pathologist at several hospitals, including the Royal Alexandra Hospital for Infectious Diseases. He also co-authored a medical textbook: *A Text-Book of Pathology for Students of Medicine*, published in 1912. A man with an adventurous mindset, McCrae became a field surgeon with the Canadian Expeditionary Force (CEF) and British forces on the Western Front in the First World War. During this service, he managed a field hospital taking in casualties from the Second Battle of Ypres, a job requiring the utmost strength of character to endure mentally. In a letter to his mother he remembered:

> For seventeen days and seventeen nights none of us have had our clothes off, nor our boots even, except occasionally. In all that time while I was awake, gunfire and rifle fire never ceased for sixty seconds … And behind it all was the constant background of the sights of the dead, the wounded, the maimed, and a terrible anxiety lest the line should give way.

McCrae also suffered personal loss during the battle – his friend and his former student Lieutenant Alexis Helmer was killed in action. McCrae conducted the burial service himself, but during this time he also noticed the red poppies growing obstinately throughout the Flanders landscape. Being a man of literary talents, the poppies and his dead friend began to stir a poetic vision that would move generations to come.

The origins of McCrae's poem 'In Flanders Fields' are uncertain, in terms of when and where he first composed it, but he became convinced of its merit and spent several months working it into shape. He eventually submitted it to *The Spectator* magazine, but it was rejected. Yet his next submission, to the redoubtable *Punch*, was accepted, and it was published on 8 December 1915. Here is the poem in full:

> In Flanders fields the poppies blow
> Between the crosses, row on row,
> That mark our place; and in the sky
> The larks, still bravely singing, fly
> Scarce heard amid the guns below.
>
> We are the Dead. Short days ago
> We lived, felt dawn, saw sunset glow,
> Loved and were loved, and now we lie
> In Flanders fields.

> Take up our quarrel with the foe:
> To you from failing hands we throw
> The torch; be yours to hold it high.
> If ye break faith with us who die
> We shall not sleep, though poppies grow
> In Flanders fields.

The poem manages to walk that fine line between patriotism and grief, mourning and resilience. The opening image, of the poppies scattered amongst the graves, seems to hold out promise of some beauty in a dark world, although the statement 'We are the Dead' at the beginning of the second stanza has a disturbing, blunt effect. By the end of poem, the poppy and the dead are inextricably intertwined, as if the flower makes visible the absence of the fallen.

'In Flanders Fields' had an enormous effect on the reading public. It was translated into dozens of languages and achieved global distribution. The poem was applied in political campaigns in Canada, and was given out as encouragement to British and, later, US soldiers fighting on the Western Front. It was also utilised persuasively in campaigns to get the public to purchase war bonds. More importantly, such was the power of the poem that it endured the war years to become a staple classic of the particular genre known as 'war poetry'. (As the author was writing this book, even his teenage daughter instantly recognised the poem when she caught a glance of it on the screen.)

Not everyone has been impressed with 'In Flanders Fields'. The patriotism it contains, especially in the last stanza, often strikes as jingoism to the modern ear, a tool for recruiting more men and sending them to the grinding mill of the Western Front. Yet for the purposes of our narrative here, one effect is key – it began the development of the Remembrance Poppy.

MOINA MICHAEL AND THE CREATION OF THE POPPY

Born in Good Hope, Georgia, USA, on 15 August 1869, Moina Belle Michael may seem an unlikely figure to intersect with our narrative of the Remembrance Poppy. She was a highly educated woman, and by the outbreak of war in Europe in 1914 she was a professor at the University of Georgia. Michael was also a passionate humanitarian, and as the war progressed she devoted more of her time to working for the Young Women's Christian Association, helping to ready workers for overseas service. In her autobiography, *The Miracle Flower: The Story of the Flanders Fields Memorial Poppy* (1941), Michael explained how, when in New York City on

BRITISH CASUALTIES ON THE WESTERN FRONT, JULY–DECEMBER 1916

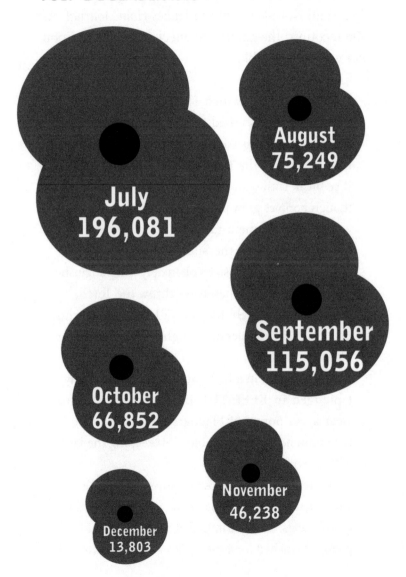

July
196,081

August
75,249

September
115,056

October
66,852

November
46,238

December
13,803

9 November 1918, with the Armistice just two days away, she came across McCrae's poem (then titled 'We Shall Not Sleep') in the *Ladies Home Journal*. As she recounts, the emotional effect of the poem upon her was considerable:

I read the poem, which I had read many times previously, and studied its graphic picturization. The last verse transfixed me — 'To you from failing hands we throw the Torch; be yours to hold it high. If ye break faith with us who die, we shall not sleep, though poppies grow in Flanders Fields'.

This was for me a full spiritual experience. It seemed as though the silent voices again were vocal, whispering, in sighs of anxiety unto anguish, 'To you from failing hands we throw the Torch; be yours to hold it high. If ye break faith with us who die we shall not sleep, though poppies grow in Flanders Fields'.

Alone, again, in a high moment of white resolve I pledged to KEEP THE FAITH and always to wear a red poppy of Flanders Fields as a sign of remembrance and the emblem of 'keeping the faith with all who died'.

In hectic times as were those times, great emotional impacts may be obliterated by succeeding greater ones. So I felt impelled to make note of my pledge. I reached for a used yellow envelope, turned

the blank side up and hastily scribbled my pledge to
keep the faith with all who died.

Moina Michael, *The Miracle Flower: The Story of the*
Flanders Fields Memorial Poppy, 1941

In this vivid moment, Michael crystallised the idea
for the Remembrance Poppy. (McCrae himself was no
longer alive by this time – he had died of pneumonia
on 28 January 1918.) She quickly went out and
acquired all the artificial red poppies she could find in
the Wanamaker's department store, and began to sell
them. It was the beginning of a concerted campaign to
make the poppy a national commemorative symbol.
Her vision was for a single national motif, albeit one
that could be reproduced in various different forms,
to act as a reminder of all those lost in the war. In
December 1918 she worked with a designer, Lee
Keedick, who helped her produce a final motif. It
featured a poppy, coloured with all the hues of the
Allied flags, intertwined with a Torch of Liberty. With
this design in hand, Michael strode on tirelessly,
pushing for national adoption, but two years of effort
did not seem to advance her cause significantly.

Then came a breakthrough. In August 1920,
Michael convinced the Georgia Department of the
American Legion (a US veterans' organisation) to
adopt the Memorial Poppy as its symbol, albeit
without the Torch of Liberty motif. This in turn,

'WE SHALL KEEP THE FAITH'

Moina Michael wrote 'We Shall Keep the Faith' in response to her reading of McCrae's 'We Shall Not Sleep'/'In Flanders Fields':

Oh! you who sleep in Flanders Fields,
Sleep sweet – to rise anew!
We caught the torch you threw
And holding high, we keep the Faith
With All who died.

We cherish, too, the poppy red
That grows on fields where valor led;
It seems to signal to the skies
That blood of heroes never dies,
But lends a lustre to the red
Of the flower that blooms above the dead
In Flanders Fields.

And now the Torch and Poppy Red
We wear in honor of our dead.
Fear not that ye have died for naught;
We'll teach the lesson that ye wrought
In Flanders Fields.
In Flanders Fields we fought.

Moina Michael

at the National American Legion convention in Cleveland on 29 September 1920, led to the Memorial Poppy being adopted as a country-wide symbol of remembrance, with the idea that American Legion members and supportive members of the public would wear the poppy annually on Armistice Day, 11 November. Michael had achieved her goal, but now the Memorial Poppy was about to spread internationally.

FURTHER AFIELD

A key person present at the National American Legion convention in 1920 was a member of the French YWCA, Madame Anna E. Guérin. Like Michael, she found the vision of the Memorial Poppy one that could not be ignored. In particular, she saw possibilities for the sale of large numbers of artificial poppies in her home country, the proceeds going towards helping those who were still suffering from the after-effects of war, particularly orphaned children. Once back in France, she straight away set about producing the fabric poppies for sale. But her ambitions were actually international, and she also began travelling to other countries, or sent representatives, to drive the concept of the Memorial Poppy.

PLACES IN WHICH BRITAIN HAS FOUGHT WARS SINCE 1945

Northern
Ireland
(1969–98)

Cyprus (1955–59)
Palestine (1922–48)
Suez (1956)
Egypt (1951–53)
Iraq (2003–09)
Oman and Dhofar (1962–75)
Aden (1963–67)
Sierra Leone (2000)
Kenya (1952–60)
Falkland Islands
(1982)

Afghanistan (2001–Present)

Persian Gulf/
Kuwait (1990–91)

Yangtze River (1949)

Korea (1950–53)

Malaya (1948–60)

Borneo (1962–66)

WHAT THE POPPY MEANS

Mike Wilson, Director of Operations, County Durham Emergency Medical Services:

I have always worn my poppy with pride, as a symbol of remembrance for those that have made the ultimate sacrifice, our fallen. This symbol has now become even more poignant following the death of my identical twin brother, Lance Corporal David Wilson, in Iraq in 2008. In the following years The Royal British Legion helped and supported our family through tough times, assisting us through David's inquest in February this year. The Poppy Appeal is not only a way of remembering our fallen, but it is also a vital way in which we can all support the important work of The Royal British Legion. So let's all wear our poppy with pride and remember.

(The Royal British Legion, 2014)

In 1921 alone, Guérin travelled to Australia, Canada, New Zealand and Britain, and the audiences there proved more than open to the idea of the Memorial Poppy. In the same year that millions of poppies were sold across the United States, the Great War Veterans Association of Canada also adopted the poppy as its national emblem of remembrance, on 5 July 1921. The next stop on Guérin's itinerary was Great Britain, and she sought to meet with none other than Field Marshal Douglas Haig.

Haig is now a rather ambiguous figure in relation to the First World War, blamed by many for directly elevating the numbers of British and Empire casualties during the First World War. Yet his role in the support of post-war veterans was crucial. He was genuinely appalled at the financial hardship experienced by many veterans back on the streets of Britain, so Guérin's approaches found a receptive ear. Haig was also the president of The British Legion, founded in 1921 through the fusion of four organisations: the Comrades of the Great War, the National Association of Discharged Sailors and Soldiers, the National Federation of Discharged and Demobilized Sailors and Soldiers, and the Officers' Association.

The idea of a Remembrance Poppy, sold as a way to generate funds for veterans, was quickly embraced by Haig with the support of The British Legion. To handle the proceeds of the sales, Haig established the

Earl Haig Fund, which also included the Earl Haig Fund Scotland. The Poppy Factory, manned by five disabled veterans, was founded in 1922 in Old Kent Road, South London. This factory quickly proved too small for the purpose, and in 1926 the production line moved to the disused Lansdown Brewery in Petersham Road, Richmond, with workforce housing built opposite. That same year, Countess Dorothy Haig, Earl Haig's wife, founded a similar Poppy Factory in Edinburgh. (The role of the Haig Fund is the reason that for many years the black plastic button in the centre of the Remembrance Poppy bore the words 'Haig Fund'.)

The first British Legion Poppy Day appeal began in the autumn of 1921, with hundreds of thousands of French-made poppies (for this year) selling across the country. But Britain's imperial connections and the ceaseless energies of Madame Guérin meant that the Remembrance Poppy soon spread further afield – Australia also launched its first poppy appeal in 1921, with the official recognition that the poppy would be worn every year on 11 November. New Zealand followed suit in 1922. In the space of four years, and largely on account of the vision of two women – one American and one French – the United States, Canada, Britain, France, Australia and New Zealand had adopted what we now call the Remembrance Poppy, establishing national traditions that survive to this day.

THE MODERN POPPY

One of the striking things about the Remembrance Poppy is its durability. Founded in the emotional aftermath of a world war, it could have gradually withered on the vine as time marched on and interest waned. Obviously, the fact that the First World War was following just over two decades later by an even larger world war kept the idea of remembrance utterly relevant, as did Britain's numerous post-war conflicts. There have been changes, particularly in terms of the poppy's administration. For example, soon after the launch of the Poppy Appeal in the UK, The British Legion took over responsibility from the Officers' Association for running the annual campaign, while in Scotland the Officers' Association Scotland ran its own appeal independently. Then in 1954, the Earl Haig Fund Scotland was established as a stand-alone charity, albeit renamed in 2006 as the Poppy Appeal Scotland. Meanwhile The British Legion received a royal charter in 1978, to become The Royal British Legion. In 2011, the Poppy Appeal Scotland merged with The Royal British Legion, although it continues to operate as a separate charity.

And what of the Remembrance Poppy itself? Richmond and Edinburgh remain the poppy's centres of production. The Richmond factory alone produces 34–45 million poppies each year, the whole operation run primarily by a dedicated team of veterans. The poppy is manufactured in a wide range of formats, so alongside the traditional paper and plastic version sit silk poppies, metallic pins, complete wreaths, wooden crosses, crescents, stars and Khandas, and shopping bags. Sold by thousands of volunteers across the country every year, the poppies raise millions of pounds for the causes of veterans and their families. (More about veteran support is described in Chapter 5.) The contribution of this simple item to the welfare of thousands of deserving people is therefore inestimable.

But apart from the vital fundraising performed by the Poppy Appeal every year, it has a deeper purpose. Although it was born from the bitter aftermath of a world war, the poppy has largely avoided becoming just a symbol of British, Commonwealth or American commemoration. It is not jingoistic or threatening (a danger of any national symbol), but instead compels entire nations to stop and reflect upon the human cost of war, both to themselves and to their former enemies. War is a complex and harrowing issue, and one that resists moral, political or philosophical simplicities. Nor must we try to gloss over what it is that soldiers are compelled to do in war. Violence is always a terrible act, whether it is dressed up in uniform or not. Many soldiers are afflicted with the effects of post-traumatic stress disorder (PTSD) precisely because the things they were obliged to perform don't square easily with their fundamental humanity. The Remembrance Poppy does not attempt to glorify or romanticise conflict, but instead, at least once a year, obliges us to face and think about the consequences of war, past, present and future.

WHAT THE POPPY MEANS

Sarah Barton, Volunteer,
The Royal British Legion:

I wear my poppy with pride. Volunteering for The Royal British Legion is a fantastic and worthwhile experience and something that I truly believe in. I have now been a volunteer for over two years. My granddad joined the 44 Royal Marine Commandos in 1943 and I remember the stories he used to tell me as a child of his experiences serving in Burma. He was a member of The Royal British Legion and Burma Star Association until his death in 2005. When leaving the Armed Forces, ex-Servicemen and Women are faced with many issues such as isolation, unemployment, poverty, homelessness, low self-esteem, mental health issues etc. and it is important to have a charity such as The Royal British Legion to support them in overcoming these issues. This is why it is crucial to have the Poppy Appeal because without this they would not be able to get the full support they need in order to build a better future for themselves.

(The Royal British Legion, 2014)

3. NOT FORGOTTEN

WALK AROUND THE centre of any village or town in Britain and you are almost guaranteed to come across a war memorial. They range from the humble – small, now-faded metal plaques bolted to the walls of civic buildings – to majestic cenotaphs and statues, towering memorials to the war dead of generations past. We have become familiar with such features, hastening past them while our daily lives consume our attention. Yet should we stop, just for a moment, and reflect upon what they represent both historically and personally, then it becomes clear that they are extraordinary cultural landmarks.

Take, for example, the war memorial that adorns just one, very particular, location – Woking Post Office. A simple marble plaque on a wall explains that it is 'Erected to the Memory of Officers of Woking Post Office who gave their lives in the Great War'. It then goes on to list the names and formations of the dead:

Allen W.G. – Grenadier Guards
Bruce V.E. – Leading Seaman RFR
Coles C.T. – PO Rifles
Goldsmith F.C. – East Kent Regt
Keene T.G. – RE Sigs
Orr D.W. – PO Rifles
Riddiford W.B. – PO Rifles
Urquhart I. – MT RFA
Warner W.J. – RGA
Wise A.J. – Tank Corps

Reflection reveals what an extraordinary historical statement is made by this memorial. A single place of work – a post office in the borough of Woking – lost no fewer than ten of its workers in the years 1914–18. The total staff of the post office would have been unlikely to number more than a few dozen, so their deaths would have sent emotional trauma rippling through the building with every new War Office telegram that arrived. Beyond the walls of the post office, each death would then punch a hole through the lives of wives, mothers, fathers, sons, daughters; people for whom these names represented humans at the centre of their lives. The war memorial is not just a list of names; it is a testimony to grief on a huge scale.

Of course, that scale gets even bigger depending on the memorial you visit. In terms of the First

World War, the human loss is conveyed with almost vertiginous effect by the cemeteries and memorials of Belgium and France. The Commonwealth War Graves Commission (CWGC) tends, with laudable diligence, to such sites across the world, but even their neatness and peace cannot mask the horror of what they represent. For example, the Tyne Cot cemetery in Belgian Flanders is today the largest Commonwealth cemetery in the world. It contains, in serried, silent ranks, the graves of 11,956 Commonwealth servicemen, 8,369 of them unidentified. To compound the power of this sight, the Tyne Cot Memorial to the Missing then adds the names of a further 35,000 officers and men whose bodies were not recovered. In nearby Ypres also stands the majestic Menin Gate Memorial to the Missing; its cavernous Hall of Memory features dozens of stone panels, on which are carved the names of 54,896 Commonwealth soldiers who died in Flanders. So, in total, these two locations remember more than 100,000 war dead, the deaths incurred in one particular sector of the Western Front in four years of terrible bloodshed.

It is a truism that deaths numbering in the tens of thousands can often have less emotional impact than the death of a single person. And yet, each name given on a wall, each grave tended, does indeed connect to a real person, an individual who once had a beating heart and breathing lungs, and who wondered whether he would reach the end of the day alive.

THE INSTINCT TO REMEMBER

Memorials to wars have always been with us, but their nature has changed profoundly over time. Back in antiquity, we find numerous monumental works celebrating victories (rather fewer remembering defeats), often sculpted or cast to glorify the exploits of a campaigning empire. Imperial Rome was replete with them, and some still stand defiantly today in that city – Trajan's Column is the most well-known, consisting of 32 tons of marble standing 98ft (30m) high, around which winds 623ft (190m) of frieze depicting scenes of war between the Romans and the Dacians (CE 101–102 and CE 105–106). Trajan's Column went on to inspire dozens of victory columns around the world, but the other popular format for war memorials was the triumphal arch. Triumphal arches not only provided plenty of space for patriotic verses, they also created an avenue through which a victorious army could march in full view of the gathered masses – they were the ultimate public relations monument. Once again, Rome proliferates with such arches, typically

COMMONWEALTH WAR GRAVES COMMISSION – GRAVES AND MEMORIALS ATTENDED (BRITAIN AND COMMONWEALTH)

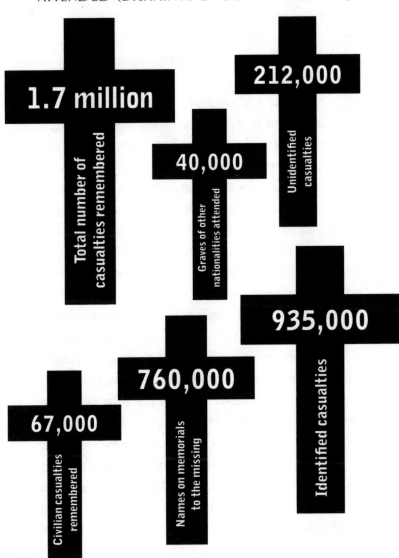

1.7 million
Total number of casualties remembered

212,000
Unidentified casualties

40,000
Graves of other nationalities attended

935,000
Identified casualties

760,000
Names on memorials to the missing

67,000
Civilian casualties remembered

labelled with the name of the emperor who secured the victory; great examples include the Arch of Titus and the Arch of Constantine. Another classical way of remembering a war, or at least a victory, was simply to carve an overbearing statue of the relevant ruler or commander, and stand it portentously in a public place. During the fifth century BCE and subsequently, for example, Athens would have had more than its fair share of statues of Pericles, who led Athens during the first two years of the Peloponnesian War (431–404 BCE).

One notable aspect of these early monuments is that the focus is very much on State and imperial power, or the acts of the great commanders. The efforts and sacrifices of the humble soldier, although depicted in battle images, are largely subjugated under the greater theme of national duty. This trend continues in war memorials right up to the nineteenth century. Throughout the medieval period, wars and victories have been remembered through imposing and rather alienating statuary and monuments, such as the neoclassical Arc de Triomphe in Paris, on which are listed French victories in the Revolutionary and Napoleonic Wars plus the names of 660 significant individuals (mostly generals) who died during the same period. In Britain (as throughout Europe), city centres are often graced with the figures of commanders on horseback or in suitable martial stance (such as Nelson's Column) in London, and cathedrals frequently bear marble victory plaques or proudly display tattered regimental colours retrieved from the battlefield.

During the nineteenth and early twentieth century, we see the first hints of battle memorials becoming increasingly focused on the sacrifices of the rank and file. In Europe and the United States, more regimental and unit memorials were built after conflicts such as the American Civil War, Franco-Prussian War and Boer War. For example, a large memorial column was erected on Coombe Hill, near Wendover in the UK, in 1904. It was expressly focused on remembering the war dead of Buckinghamshire in the Boer War, listing their names solemnly on a memorial plaque.

It was the First World War that truly galvanised the spread of more personalised war memorials in the UK. Most of these memorials were erected after the conflict, from 1918 to about 1932. During this period, the British people were still trying to come to grips with the scale of the human loss that had befallen the nation. Furthermore, repatriation of the dead was not a standard practice during the conflict; most of the dead were buried where they fell or in improvised cemeteries near the frontline, and were later (when possible, bearing in mind the thousands of men who remained missing) disinterred and moved to concentrated war cemeteries. For millions of people back in Britain, what this meant was that they had no grave to visit. Therefore public memorials were the only tangible way to create a visible focus for their grief, and to bring the dead back into the community.

As a result, war memorials proliferated. Furthermore, Britain established rites of remembrance that would unify the nation in its loss. The first step was to set a specific day of commemoration. The natural choice was 11 November. For on that day – the eleventh day of the eleventh month – the guns fell silent on the Western Front, as the Armistice came into effect. The 1919 anniversary of this day was earmarked as Armistice Day, and it was to be both a day of remembrance plus a celebration of the victory that had been so hard won. To this day, a period of silence is observed nationally and in many countries around the world at 11 a.m. on 11 November, but the main UK day of remembrance was moved to the second Sunday in the month, known as 'Remembrance Sunday'.

In London, the official State participation in Remembrance Sunday had a new focal point. The Cenotaph monument, set on Whitehall, was designed by the renowned architect Sir Edwin Landseer Lutyens. It was initially a temporary wood and marble structure, erected for the London Victory

Parade on 19 July 1919. (This was held to celebrate the signing of the Treaty of Versailles on 28 June.) After the event, the base of the memorial accrued various wreaths and tokens of remembrance, so a campaign gathered pace to keep the Cenotaph, but replace the temporary structure with a permanent stone edifice, albeit one keeping faithfully to the original design. Thus the Cenotaph was rebuilt from Portland Stone between 1919 and 1920, and this is the memorial that stands today, unveiled by King George V on 11 November 1920.

The Cenotaph has a strangely austere quality to it. Many other memorials around the UK personalise the British soldier in statuary, depicting figures of men carved or cast with astonishing attention to detail in terms of expression, kit and weaponry. The Cenotaph, by contrast, is monolithic, a huge column of stone, 35ft (11m) high and topped by the gaunt cenotaph (an empty tomb). At each end is a wreath, 5ft (1.5m) in diameter, displaying the words 'The Glorious Dead' below, while above are the dates of the First World War in Roman numerals (1914 – MCMXIV; 1919 – MCMXIX). Flags representing the various arms of service are displayed on either side of the monument.

Since 1919, the Cenotaph has been the focus of the National Service of Remembrance, typically attended by key members of the government and royal family, plus visiting foreign dignitaries. At first it was very much a national event, concentrating exclusively on the British war dead, a focus refreshed by the additional third of a million dead suffered during the Second World War. Yet time has changed the perspective somewhat. In 1980, it was decided that Remembrance Sunday should properly be an act of remembrance for all those who have died in conflict, regardless of their nationality or the war in which they lost their lives.

Of course, the Cenotaph is not the only national-level war memorial in England, Scotland, Wales and Northern Ireland. Unveiled on 12 October 2007, the Armed Forces Memorial near Lichfield in Staffordshire remembers the 16,000 British soldiers killed in conflicts post-1945. In Northern Ireland, Belfast has its own Cenotaph, set in a Garden of Remembrance. In Alexandra Gardens, Cardiff, there is the Welsh National War Memorial designed by Sir Ninian Comper and unveiled in June 1928. On the outer frieze of the colonnaded design is the Welsh inscription: I FEIBION CYMRU A RODDES EU BYWYD DROS EI GWLAD YN RHYFEL MCMXVIII, which translates as 'To the sons of Wales who gave their lives for their country in the War 1918.' In Scotland, the Scottish National War Memorial sits in the stunning location of Edinburgh Castle, towering over the city. Rolls of Honour inside the memorial list the names of nearly 200,000 Scottish people who died in the two world wars.

Space does not allow us here to list many of the other great memorials that stretch throughout our land. The bulk of them date from the First World War years and the 1920s–30s, as the act of war-memorial building was not as enthusiastically embraced following the Second World War. (What we often find is that the names of those killed in the Second World War are added to the monument from the previous conflict.) Each ceremony on Remembrance Sunday has its own power and conviction, yet there are some features of the service that unite the country in its reflection upon conflict.

SOME FAMOUS INTERNATIONAL WAR MEMORIALS

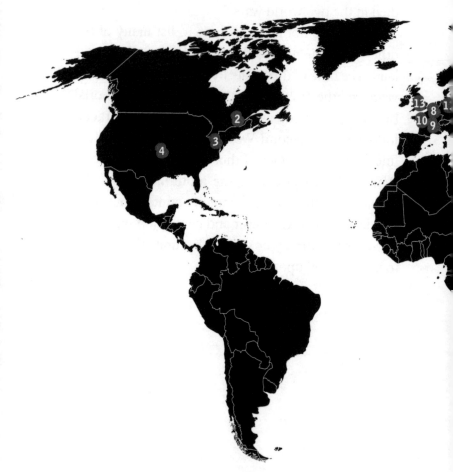

1. Unknown Soldier Memorial – Cairo, Egypt
2. National War Memorial – Ottawa, Canada
3. Vietnam Veterans Memorial Wall – Washington DC, USA
4. Liberty Memorial – Kansas City, USA
5. Monument to the People's Heroes – Beijing, China
6. India Gate – New Delhi, India
7. Yasukuni Shrine – Tokyo, Japan

8. Menin Gate Memorial to the Missing – Ypres, Belgium
9. Douaument Ossuary – Douaumont, France
10. Thiepval Memorial to the Missing of the Somme
11. Monument of the Battle of Nations – Leipzig, Germany
12. Mamayev Kurgan – Volgograd, Russia
13. The Cenotaph – London, UK
14. ANZAC War Memorial – Sydney, Australia

POWERFUL WORDS, POWERFUL SILENCE

In 1914, as the first dreadful casualty lists began to flow back to Britain from France and Belgium, the poet Robert Laurence Binyon composed a verse entitled 'For the Fallen', which was published in *The Times* in September. Although Binyon is likely to have been proud of the verse, he would have had little inkling at that early stage of the war how influential parts of the poem would become. In full, his poem read:

For the Fallen

With proud thanksgiving, a mother for her children,
England mourns for her dead across the sea.
Flesh of her flesh they were, spirit of her spirit,
Fallen in the cause of the free.

Solemn the drums thrill; Death august and royal
Sings sorrow up into immortal spheres.
There is music in the midst of desolation
And a glory that shines upon our tears.

They went with songs to the battle, they were young,
Straight of limb, true of eye, steady and aglow.

They were staunch to the end against odds uncounted,
They fell with their faces to the foe.

They shall grow not old, as we that are left grow old:
Age shall not weary them, nor the years condemn.
At the going down of the sun and in the morning
We will remember them.

They mingle not with their laughing comrades again;
They sit no more at familiar tables of home;
They have no lot in our labour of the day-time;
They sleep beyond England's foam.

But where our desires are and our hopes profound,
Felt as a well-spring that is hidden from sight,
To the innermost heart of their own land they are
known
As the stars are known to the Night;

As the stars that shall be bright when we are dust,
Moving in marches upon the heavenly plain,
As the stars that are starry in the time of our darkness,
To the end, to the end, they remain.

Robert Laurence Binyon

To see the poem complete, rather than just focus on the well-known fourth stanza, brings a sense of the gulf between the attitudes to war in 1914 and those that prevailed just a few years later. The poem is undoubtedly patriotic, seeing a nobility and grandeur in conflict that had been largely purged by 1918. The soldiers advancing to meet their fates are 'straight', 'true' and 'steady' – any suggestion of fear is absent. And yet, there are moments of transcendent beauty in this poem, especially the fourth stanza. Such was the emotive power of this passage that it was separated from the rest of the poem to become the familiar Ode of Remembrance, still read out with solemnity at remembrance services in the UK, Australia, New Zealand and other Commonwealth nations. It is an acutely moving passage, combining eternity and mortality and a clear statement of intent by those who are alive: 'We will remember them'. Although the overall poem from which it came does not chime well with the modern age, Binyon nevertheless left a powerful and timeless verse that is likely to endure for decades, if not centuries.

In the remembrance services, Binyon's verse sits next to a period of two minutes' silence, held in respect of the world's war dead. For visitors to the UK who do not have this tradition, the experience can be moving, even startling. At 11 a.m. on 11 November (or on the following Sunday), much of the country simply stops, comes to its feet, and stands with heads bowed in silence for a period of two minutes. Businesses, schools, shopping centres, sports fixtures, government buildings – all make this unique gesture every year, a reflective break in the middle of a bustling day.

The idea of the two-minute silence was put forward by Australian journalist Edward George Honey in a letter to *The Times* in May 1919. It was embraced by the public, government and royalty, although there was initially some debate about the appropriate period for which silence had to be held. Five minutes was the initial suggestion, but this was felt to be too long, and the alternative one minute too short. Hence the two-minute silence was adopted, and on 7 November 1919, King George V declared that:

At the hour when the Armistice comes into force, the eleventh hour of the eleventh day of the eleventh month, there may be for the brief space of two minutes a complete suspension of all our normal activities … so that in perfect stillness, the thoughts of everyone may be concentrated on reverent remembrance of the glorious dead.

THE LAST POST

'The Last Post' is a haunting bugle or trumpet call heard during British and Commonwealth Remembrance Day services, and at other commemorative events throughout the year. Its origins lie back in the British Army of the seventeenth century, when the call was played at the end of the day to signal that night sentries were at their posts and the day was effectively over. ('The First Post' signalled the start of an officer's evening inspections.) In time, the call was incorporated into military funerals and acts of remembrance. Since 1928 it has also been played every day at 8 p.m. at the Menin Gate war memorial in Ieper (Ypres) in Belgium.

WAR GRAVES

Even today, after a century of time has passed, the battlefields of the First World War keep relinquishing the dead. In 2007–08, for example, mass burial pits that had lain undisturbed for ninety years were discovered on the outskirts of Fromelles in northern France. They contained the bodies of 250 Commonwealth soldiers (mostly Australians) who had been killed in the Battle of Fromelles (a subsidiary operation to the Battle of the Somme) on 19 July 1916, and were subsequently buried by the Germans in communal graves.

Upon the discovery of the bodies, the Commonwealth War Graves Commission (CWGC) began attempting to identify the dead, analysing the surviving artefacts around the bodies and using modern DNA analysis techniques. Ultimately, the bodies consisted of 205 Australians (ninety-six of whom the CWGC identified by name) plus three British soldiers and the rest 'unknowns'. A special cemetery was constructed in 2009–10, known as the Fromelles (Pheasant Wood) Military Cemetery, and the bodies were eventually laid to rest with full military honours.

Military cemeteries are unique places of remembrance. Some are relatively small, tucked away in distant locations. The Gravesend Military Cemetery in Bridgetown, Barbados, for example, is a CWGC cemetery containing the bodies of just nine individuals, all killed in action between 1942 and 1944. At the other end of the extreme are the huge, almost disorientating cemeteries and memorials in Western Europe, of which the following are representative. The Fricourt German War Cemetery contains the bodies of 17,027 German soldiers, while the Douamont Ossuary on the Verdun battlefield site contains the bones of more than 130,000 unidentified soldiers, the remains taken from the devastating battle of 1916. The Meuse-Argonne American Cemetery and Memorial, the largest American burial site in Europe, has 14,246 graves spread over 130 acres (52 hectares). The huge Thiepval Memorial to the Missing displays the names of 73,357 British and Allied soldiers who died in the Somme area between 1916 and 1918, but who have no official grave.

The cemeteries and memorials listed are just a handful from one particular conflict. In fact, there are thousands of military cemeteries around the world, some kept with a military eye for cleanliness and detail, others neglected and forgotten beneath overgrown foliage. For the British and Commonwealth countries, the job of maintaining the war cemeteries falls to the CWGC.

COMMONWEALTH WAR GRAVES COMMISSION – KEY FACTS

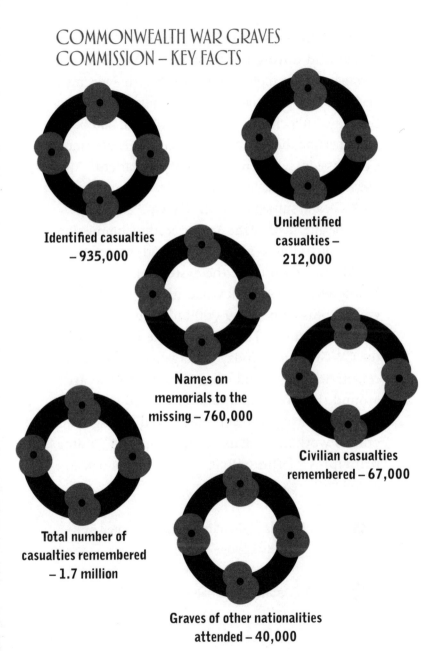

Identified casualties – 935,000

Unidentified casualties – 212,000

Names on memorials to the missing – 760,000

Civilian casualties remembered – 67,000

Total number of casualties remembered – 1.7 million

Graves of other nationalities attended – 40,000

The CWGC was the vision of one man, Sir Fabian Ware, who during the First World War was the commander of a mobile unit of the British Red Cross. Seeing at first hand the levels of casualties, and noting the frequently chaotic processes of burial and body identification, he established the Graves Registration Commission, which received a royal charter in May 1917 to become the Imperial War Graves Commission (IWGC), and subsequently the CWGC.

In the aftermath of the Armistice, the Commission set about trying to identify the dead, record their details and rationalise the system of cemeteries. By the end of 1918 they had identified 587,000 graves, plus named 559,000 individuals who had no known grave. This was just the beginning of the CWGC's work. Today the organisation cares for cemeteries, graves and memorials in 153 countries around the world, at a total of 23,000 locations. The number of war dead represented through this critical work now totals 1.7 million. The guiding principles of the CWGC in all this work are as follows:

- Each of the dead should be commemorated by a name on the headstone or memorial

- Headstones and memorials should be permanent

- Headstones should be uniform

- There should be no distinction made on account of military or civil rank, race or creed.

The two central themes of this list are 'permanence' and 'equality'. Unlike the military memorials of centuries past, the CWGC cemeteries and memorials recognise that all the soldiers who died deserve enduring respect, regardless of rank or position.

TOMB OF THE UNKNOWN SOLDIER

One of the many tragedies of the First World War was that so many of the war dead found no permanent grave. Many were hastily buried in crude holes cut into active battlefields, and their rudimentary grave markers were subsequently lost or destroyed in the confusion of action. Thousands were buried in communal graves, their identities often lost in the mass of humanity they lay amongst. Others simply went 'missing', many destroyed beyond recognition by high explosive.

For the families of these men and women, the tragedy of their loss was compounded by the complete absence of a grave over which to mourn. This truth was recognised by one Reverend David Railton, a British clergyman serving on the Western Front in 1916, but in a back garden at Armentieres, France, he saw a possible solution. There stood a crude cross bearing the simple words 'An Unknown British Soldier'. The sight left an impression on Railton, and in 1920, with the war over, he wrote to the Dean of Westminster Abbey, Herby Ryle, suggesting that a single tomb be established in the Abbey containing the body of one unidentified British soldier. Thus placed, the soldier would serve almost

REMEMBERING THE UNKNOWN SOLDIER

Below is part of the eulogy delivered by the Australian Prime Minister, Paul Keating, at the funeral service of the Unknown Australian Soldier, 11 November 1993:

We do not know this Australian's name and we never will. We do not know his rank or his battalion. We do not know where he was born, nor precisely how and when he died. We do not know where in Australia he had made his home or when he left it for the battlefields of Europe. We do not know his age or his circumstances – whether he was from the city or the bush; what occupation he left to become a soldier; what religion, if he had a religion; if he was married or single. We do not know who loved him or whom he loved. If he had children we do not know who they are. His family is lost to us as he was lost to them. We will never know who this Australian was.

Yet he has always been among those whom we have honoured. We know that he was one of the 45,000 Australians who died on the Western Front. One of the 416,000 Australians who volunteered for service in the First World War. One of the 324,000 Australians who served overseas in that war and one of the 60,000 Australians who died on foreign soil. One of the 100,000 Australians who have died in wars this century. He is all of them. And he is one of us.

as the national representative for all the missing and unidentified dead.

The suggestion (which had also been made by the *Daily Express* newspaper) was adopted by the British Government, and plans for the internment were made. However, there was the sensitive issue of how to select the body. The solution was to gather a number of unidentified remains from various former battlefields and place them on stretchers in a chapel at Saint-Pol-sur-Ternoise near Arras, on the night of 7 November 1920. Two officers, Brigadier-General L.J. Wyatt and Lieutenant-Colonel E.A.S. Gell of the Directorate of Graves Registration, later visited the chapel alone, where Brigadier-General Wyatt selected one of the bodies simply by placing his hand on it. This process was followed to ensure that considerations of rank, birth, politics and other factors did not feature in the selection.

The journey of the body to its final resting place in Westminster Abbey on 11 November 1920 was a humbling sight, the casket drawn through the streets of London on a horse-drawn gun carriage, thousands of onlookers completely silent at its passage. It stopped before the Cenotaph, which then received its unveiling, before journeying on to the Abbey, where the casket was interred in the far western end of the nave, buried in soil actually brought from the battlefields. At the same time, an

INSCRIPTION ON THE TOMB
OF THE UNKNOWN WARRIOR,
WESTMINSTER ABBEY

BENEATH THIS STONE RESTS THE BODY
OF A BRITISH WARRIOR
UNKNOWN BY NAME OR RANK
BROUGHT FROM FRANCE TO LIE AMONG
THE MOST ILLUSTRIOUS OF THE LAND
AND BURIED HERE ON ARMISTICE DAY
11 NOV: 1920, IN THE PRESENCE OF
HIS MAJESTY KING GEORGE V
HIS MINISTERS OF STATE
THE CHIEFS OF HIS FORCES
AND A VAST CONCOURSE OF THE NATION
THUS ARE COMMEMORATED THE MANY
MULTITUDES WHO DURING THE GREAT
WAR OF 1914–1918 GAVE THE MOST THAT
MAN CAN GIVE LIFE ITSELF
FOR GOD
FOR KING AND COUNTRY
FOR LOVED ONES HOME AND EMPIRE
FOR THE SACRED CAUSE OF JUSTICE AND
THE FREEDOM OF THE WORLD
THEY BURIED HIM AMONG THE KINGS BECAUSE HE
HAD DONE GOOD TOWARD GOD AND TOWARD
HIS HOUSE

unknown soldier was buried at the Arc de Triomphe in Paris, the French also making this unique act of remembrance.

Many countries around the world now have their own Tomb of the Unknown Warrior. Through graves, tombs, memorials and other means, including the Remembrance Poppy, societies have done their utmost to ensure that the thousands of men and women killed in conflict are remembered, no matter how isolated, terrified or forgotten the individual was on the day of death.

SECOND WORLD WAR LIFE EXPECTANCIES
(WORST-CASE SCENARIOS)

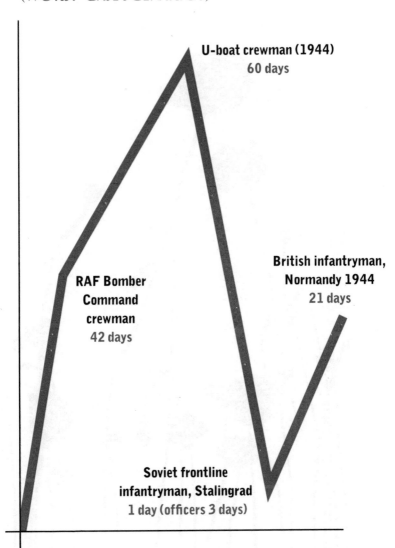

U-boat crewman (1944)
60 days

**RAF Bomber
Command
crewman
42 days**

**British infantryman,
Normandy 1944**
21 days

**Soviet frontline
infantryman, Stalingrad**
1 day (officers 3 days)

4. THEY SHALL NOT GROW OLD

ONE OF THE challenges of writing, and reading, military history is making a meaningful human connection with the individuals of the past. This is particularly a problem regarding major wars, when individuals fight and die in extremely large numbers. At the Battle of Stalingrad, for example, the best part of 1 million individuals died in the clashes of 1942–43, a figure that is simply too great to grasp on a human level. The danger is that all those who were involved with the battle become an undifferentiated mass, prey to historical platitudes and assumptions.

As an author I have spent much of my adult life reading and researching military history. During this time, I have read hundreds of first-hand accounts and non-fiction histories, visited numerous battlefields and military bases, and interviewed dozens of serving soldiers and veterans. From this research, one thing has become clear to me – military personnel are as diverse in character as the rest of the world.

One of the reasons why I am still compelled by military history is because in it you find the absolute best and the absolute worst of human character, and soldiers, sailors and airmen occupy every grade of that spectrum. We should neither put all military personnel on a pedestal, nor treat them all with suspicion. Instead, we should try to find ways in which they come alive as individuals, looking at them as much as possible through their actions and their words.

First-hand accounts are one of the best ways of making the voices of war come alive. I was first made aware of this fact through my father, Brian McNab, who was 10 years old when the Second World War began in 1939. During my youth, my father recounted an event that fascinates me to this day, if only because hundreds of thousands of people of his generation would have had similar experiences. During the Blitz of 1940–41, Brian sat out the war in relative safety on Thornes Road, Wakefield, North Yorkshire. German bombers sometimes passed overhead, but their main targets were the great industrial cities such as Leeds, Sheffield and Manchester (my father recounted seeing the glow in the night sky on the horizon as Sheffield burned). Yet with each outlying raid, the people of Wakefield still had to follow Air Raid

Precautions. For my father, his mother and his sister Jean – his father was an ARP warden so would be out on duty – this meant going next door to Mrs Clegg's house, and sitting out the night in a cold, damp and dull cellar deep beneath the ground. When the all-clear sounded, they would ascend the stairs in the morning, tired and aching.

Most nights spent in this way were completely uneventful, a fact that bred complacency. On the night of 14 March 1941, the group had been huddled down in the cellar for hours. There was no sound from above – no droning aircraft, no anti-aircraft fire in the distance, no shouted warnings. At one point, just before 10.50 p.m., the decision was made to ascend the cellar stairs and go into the living room for a good cup of tea. What they did not know was that high above was a single German Heinkel He 111 bomber. It had been heading for Sheffield with two SC 1000 1,000kg (2,200lb) high-explosive bombs, but British radar jamming had thrown off its navigation. Now, all the aircrew were concerned about was getting home, and to do that quicker they had to lighten the load. Brian takes up the story:

She [Mrs Clegg] came out with the tea … and we were saying how it had all been very quiet tonight when we heard a slow drone in the sky. It was just a gentle hum. And we wondered whether we ought to go down into the cellar again, but nothing happened so we stayed put. Then as we were sat there the droning got nearer and nearer. We felt at this point that we should go back to the cellar, but we suddenly heard a whistle in the sky, getting louder and louder. It started off right in the distance but built to a crescendo … we seemed to be listening to this, absolutely transfixed, for ages. Then it seemed as if the heavens had opened, an unbelievable roar. The windows came out. The blast threw us all forward out of the sofa into the fireplace, then hurled up back while at the same time soot came rushing out of the chimney and covered us. I would have sworn that the bomb was on our house next door …

In fact, the bombs had not hit the McNab house, as they discovered when they finally emerged from the cellar into which they fled again. Yet with just two bombs, the community had been devastated. Six neighbours had been killed, including (according to my father's memories of what his father later reported) twin infants who were discovered dead in their cots without a mark on them, just rendered white by falling plaster. A woman whom they knew personally had been decapitated. Several houses were completely demolished and the entire street was covered in a thick layer of soot, sucked out of the chimneys by the bombs' vacuum. Brian remembered finding a piece of still-warm bomb fragment stuck in their fence, having passed through the family garage and the car inside it.

This narrative has power for me because it can be attached to a real person. In turn, this reminds me that those who died were also real people, their lives abruptly snuffed out in a single random bombing in 1941. Had the German pilots not flicked the bomb release switch at the moment they did, then the two infant boys might still be alive today, and the other dead might have lived long and fruitful lives.

FAMOUS WAR PHOTOGRAPHERS

Name	Nationality	Life dates
Alexander Gardner	Scottish	1821–82
Don McCullin	British	b. 1935
James Nachtwey	American	b. 1948
Joe Rosenthal	American	1911–2006
Margaret Bourke-White	American	1904–71
Mathew Brady	American	c. 1882–96
Robert Capa	Hungarian	1913–54
Roger Fenton	British	1819–69

Examples of conflicts covered
American Civil War
Suez Crisis; Biafra; Vietnam War; Northern Ireland; Cyprus; Lebanon; Bangladesh; Syria (amongst others)
El Salvador; Nicaragua; Guatemala; Lebanon; the West Bank and Gaza; Sri Lanka; Afghanistan; Somalia; Sudan; Rwanda; South Africa; Bosnia; Chechnya; Kosovo
Second World War
Second World War; India-Pakistan Partition
American Civil War
Spanish Civil War; Second Sino-Japanese War; Second World War; 1948 Arab-Israeli War; First Indochina War
Crimean War

FRONTLINE VOICES: BATTLE OF BALACLAVA

Battlefield journalism was born in earnest during the nineteenth century. Arguably the first modern war reporter was British-Irish correspondent William Howard Russell, whose reports on the Crimean War (1853–56) gave the reading public a deeper insight into the realities of war. Here is part of his account of the most famous action of the conflict, the 'Charge of the Light Brigade', during the Battle of Balaclava on 25 October 1854:

At 11:00 our Light Cavalry Brigade rushed to the front … The Russians opened on them with guns from the redoubts on the right, with volleys of musketry and rifles.

They swept proudly past, glittering in the morning sun in all the pride and splendor of war. We could hardly believe the evidence of our senses. Surely that handful of men were not going to charge an army in position? Alas! It was but too true – their desperate valor knew no bounds, and far indeed was it removed from its so-called better part – discretion. They advanced in two lines, quickening the pace as they closed towards the enemy. A more fearful spectacle was never witnessed than by those who, without the power to aid, beheld their heroic countrymen rushing to the arms of sudden death. At the distance of 1200 yards the whole line of the enemy belched forth, from thirty iron mouths, a flood of smoke and flame through which hissed the deadly balls. Their flight was marked by instant gaps in our ranks, the dead men and horses, by steeds flying wounded or riderless across the plain. The first line was broken – it was joined by the second, they never halted or checked their speed an instant. With diminished ranks, thinned by those thirty guns, which the Russians had laid with the most deadly accuracy, with a halo of flashing steel above their heads, and with a cheer which was many a noble fellow's death cry, they flew into the smoke of the batteries; but ere they were lost from view, the plain was strewed with their bodies and with the carcasses of horses. They were exposed to an oblique fire from the batteries on the hills on both sides, as well as to a direct fire of musketry.

WINDOWS ON THE PAST

The account of the bombing in Wakefield perfectly illustrates the value of memories, original documents and first-hand accounts to understand the true nature of conflict during times of remembrance. The types of primary sources we can draw on to open these windows to the past are extremely diverse, but all make their own contribution. For example, the following is from a letter written on 28 May 1918 from one Captain R. Hulbert Dadd, 'B' Company, 5th Machine Gun Battalion, to the mother of a soldier killed in action:

> I regret very much to inform you that your son Pte. A.G. Harrison, No. 62732 of this Company was killed in action on the night of the 21st instant. Death was instantaneous and without any suffering.
>
> The Company was taking part in an attack and your son's gun team was one of these which advanced against the enemy. The attack was successful, and all guns reached and established new positions. Later in the night the enemy shelled our lines and one shell fell on your son's gun killing him and wounding a comrade.

It was impossible to get his remains away and he lies in a soldier's grave where he fell. I and the C.O. and all the Company deeply sympathise with you in your loss.

Your son always did his duty and now has given his life for his country. We all honour him, and I trust you will feel some consolation in remembering this.

His effects will reach you via the Base in due course.

The letter is a model of self-control, born no doubt from having to write such letters on numerous occasions. Some lines speak volumes. The statement that 'Death was instantaneous and without any suffering' was commonplace in such missives, wishing to spare the bereaved the distress of violent details (although of course sometimes the statement was perfectly true). The captain explains that it was impossible to retrieve his body, implying that either the attack had to press ahead with no time to collect the dead, or that the ground was lost to the enemy, or that there wasn't enough of a body left to take back to the rear. The final line about the return of the effects has an unusual poignancy; a mother would receive a box containing simple personal items, objects that just days or weeks previously had been turned in the hands of a precious son.

Letters from the frontline to loved ones back home always carry an emotional power. On one level this is because the letters were not written with the intention of publication. As the letter writer was communicating with a specific person or group of people, typically loved ones, the emotions and priorities of the writer seem more visible and real. We also often see soldiers writing letters that significantly downplay the dangers they face, to prevent their loved ones from worrying. However, on some occasions the writer has to face the issue of death openly, and express full feelings about the war in which they are involved.

John Alexander Raws was British-born and his family emigrated to Australia when he was a child. In 1915 he joined the Australian Corps, and was sent to fight on the Western Front as a junior officer. He was killed in August 1916 in the Battle of the Somme, but left behind him a striking sequence of letters to the various members of his family. The early letters are full of examples of nervous manliness, such as this one to his father, written on 12 July 1915:

I received your letter this evening, just a few minutes after I had passed the medical test for enlistment. I propose to go into camp in a week or two – probably Wednesday week, or Monday week – today fortnight. Meantime I shall study and drill.

FAMOUS BRITISH FIRST WORLD WAR POETS

Poet	Life Dates	Famous Poems
Edward Thomas	1878–1917	'In Memoriam'
Isaac Rosenberg	1890–1918	'August 1914'
Wilfred Owen	1893–1918	'Anthem for Doomed Youth'
Charles Sorley	1895–1915	'When you see millions of the mouthless dead'
Siegfried Sassoon	1886–1967	'Aftermath'
Robert Graves	1895–1985	'A dead Boche'

If I had received your letter before, father dear, it would have made no difference. My decision has not been sudden. My mind has been practically made up for a month or so – before the recruiting boom to which you refer – but I was waiting to advise you immediately everything was fixed, and I was accepted. The reduction of the standard has enabled me to get through. [Raws had been rejected for service the previous year, having failed a health evaluation.]

I hope that you will be proud to think that you have two sons – who were never fighting men, who abhor the sight of blood and cruelty and suffering of any kind, but who yet are game to go out bravely to a war forced upon them. There are many men, wealthy and strong, who should have gone before me, and have not. But can that excuse me? Not for one moment.

I do not go because I am afraid that my friends may think me a coward if I stay, but I do feel in going that in my small way I am conferring upon you and dear mother what should not be a crown of sorrow. You would not have your son, whatever else, a craven – one who would say that he thought others should go, but would himself hang back. If I prove unfit for service, well and good. But it has to be proved.

I said before that I claimed no great patriotism. No government, other than the most utterly democratic, is worth fighting for. But there are principles, and there are women, and there are standards of decency, that are worth shedding one's blood for, surely.

The sentiments in this letter reflect those of many men eager to join the war effort. Very few actually rejoiced in thoughts of violence and combat, but were still compelled to 'do their bit' for their country and community, while also avoiding the very real threat of being branded a coward. However, there is a deep shift in tone as Raws became more familiar with the realities of life on the frontline. This letter was written to a friend on 20 July 1916:

I am no more in love with war and soldiering, however, than I was when I left Melbourne, and if any of you lucky fellows – forgive me, but you are lucky – find yourselves longing to change your humdrum existence for the heroics of battle, you will find plenty of us willing to swop jobs. How we do think of home and laugh at the pettiness of our little daily annoyances! We could not sleep, we remember, because of the creaking of the pantry door, or the noise of the tramcars, or the kids playing around and making a row. Well, we can't sleep now because six shells are bursting around here every minute, and you can't get much sleep between them; Guns are belching out shells, with a most thunderous clap each time; The ground is shaking with each little explosion; I am wet, and the ground on which I rest is wet; My feet are cold: in fact, I'm all cold, with my two skimp blankets; I am covered with cold, clotted sweat, and sometimes my person is foul; I am hungry; I am annoyed because of the absurdity of war; I see no chance of anything better for tomorrow, or the day after, or the year after.

The letter here conveys a man stretched to his physical and mental breaking point. Subsequent letters frequently dwell on the theme of madness, in himself and in others, and his hatred of war builds to a fever pitch just days before he was killed, as in this letter to his brother on 12 August:

The glories of the Great Push are great, but the horrors are greater. With all I'd heard by word of mouth, with all I had imagined in my mind, I yet never conceived that war could be so dreadful. The carnage in our little sector was as bad, or worse, than that of Verdun, and yet I never saw a body buried in ten days. And when I came on the scene the whole place, trenches and all, was spread with dead. We had neither time nor space for burials, and the

FUTILITY

Move him into the sun –
Gently its touch awoke him once,
At home, whispering of fields unsown.
Always it woke him, even in France,
Until this morning and this snow.
If anything might rouse him now
The kind old sun will know.

Think how it wakes the seeds –
Woke, once, the clays of a cold star.
Are limbs so dear-achieved, are sides
Full-nerved, – still warm, – too hard to stir?
Was it for this the clay grew tall?
– O what made fatuous sunbeams toil
To break earth's sleep at all?

Wilfred Owen, 1918

wounded could not be got away. They stayed with us and died, pitifully, with us, and then they rotted. The stench of the battlefield spread for miles around. And the sight of the limbs, the mangled bodies, and stray heads.

We lived with all this for eleven days, ate and drank and fought amid it; but no, we did not sleep. Sometimes, we just fell down and became unconscious. You could not call it sleep.

The men who say they believe in war should be hung. And the men who won't come out and help us, now we're in it, are not fit for words. Had we more reinforcements up there many brave men now dead, men who stuck it and stuck it and stuck it till they died, would be alive today. Do you know that I saw with my own eyes a score of men go raving mad! I met three in 'No Man's Land' one night. Of course, we had a bad patch. But it is sad to think that one has to go back to it, and back to it, and back to it, until one is hit.

The final words in this letter are horribly prophetic, for Raws was killed just days later – he was hit by a shell on 23 August, and died instantly. The power of Raws' letters transcends the distance of time. He was just one of the millions of war dead from that conflict, but his letters present a real man in real time, responding to a human crisis enveloping him.

Since 1918, the literature and letters of war have continued to be written, new conflicts providing fresh contexts for reflection and remembrance. To read such literature does not require by any means an interest in military history, nor a desire to learn about the ways of war. Instead, it provides both a window into how humans think and behave under the most extreme circumstances, and poses the implicit question – what would you have done?

QUOTES FROM THE LETTERS OF JOHN RAWS

12 July 1915 – '… there are principles, and there are women, and there are standards of decency, that are worth shedding one's blood for, surely.'

27 May 1916 – 'We whistled and sang the Marseillaise as we tramped … And my word it was heavy walking! This is marching order.'

9 July 1916 – 'Against the front breastwork we have a step, about two feet high, upon which men stand to shoot. When there is a bombardment nearly everyone gets under this step, close in against the side.'

20 July 1916 – 'The shells are coming from all directions by the thousand, ours and theirs, but I'm resting in quite a comfy little machine gun emplacement. We hope to be out of it in a few days, thank goodness. Our losses have been heavy.'

8 August 1916 – 'I was buried twice and thrown down several times - buried with dead and dying. The ground was covered with bodies in all stages of decay and mutilation...'

12 August 1916 – 'I lost, in three days, my brother and my two best friends, and in all six out of seven of all my officer friends (perhaps a score in number) who went into the scrap - all killed.'

19 August 1916 – 'Before going in to this next affair, at the same dreadful spot, I want to tell you, so that it may be on record, that I honestly believe Goldy and many other officers were murdered on the night you know of, through the incompetence, callousness, and personal vanity of those high in authority.'

DEATH TOLLS OF MAJOR NAZI EXTERMINATION/CONCENTRATION CAMPS

Auschwitz-Birkenau – up to 1.6 million

Belzec – 601,000

Bergen-Belsen – 50,000

Buchenwald – 65,000

Chelmno – 255,000

Gross-Rosen – 105,000

Majdanek – 250,000

Mauthausen – 120,000

Sachsenhausen/Oranienberg – 105,000

Theresienstadt – 33,430

Treblinka – up to 870,000

5. A SYMBOL OF HOPE

ONE OF THE IRONIES of war is that a situation that sees the worst in human behaviour at the same time can bring out the best in people. We witness this with great clarity during the annual Poppy Appeal. Not only does this event represent a national and international act of remembrance, it also demonstrates a very practical desire to help veterans, military families and all those affected by the consequences of war. For example, some 350,000 volunteers and staff of The Royal British Legion work every year to make the Appeal possible, many of them giving up large portions of their spare time. Through their efforts, more than £40 million is raised annually, which then goes to good causes ranging from supporting bereaved families through to rehabilitating injured veterans. Numerous other organisations work throughout the UK to deliver support for soldiers (former and current) and their families, some providing specialist medical care found almost nowhere else. If anything, the presence of these organisations reminds us that the instinct to care is just as strong in humanity as the instinct to fight and destroy.

LIFE ON THE OUTSIDE

Military personnel tend to have fairly tough and resourceful personalities. They are used to high-pressure demands of a type rarely faced by those in civilian life. Mistakes in a war zone can literally result in lives lost. Combat troops also have to negotiate the prospect and actuality of killing people, an act that frequently leaves an impression on even the most hardened character.

Yet for all the mental resilience possessed by military personnel, life for them back in the civilian world can be hard, whether the return is the result of injury, the end of a term of service or being made unemployed. Life inside the forces tends to have a high degree of purpose and team loyalty, whereas in the civilian environment the bonds between people, especially in the workplace, are typically far weaker and more self-interested. A veteran can thus emerge from a world in which he manned a multimillion-pound armoured vehicle, or fought close-quarters actions with insurgent forces, into one that cares little for his past, indeed may even feel somewhat threatened by it. By consequence, the soldier can struggle to fit back into regular life, with potentially severe consequences for the soldier and his or her family.

In one sense, Britain and many other nations have often struggled to make society welcoming for its veterans. Following the world wars, huge numbers of disbanded troops returned home in a rapid timeframe, resulting in intense competition to find work. In Britain, both of those conflicts also left the UK in economic desperation, making the jobs market even tougher for many of the soldiers. After the First World War in particular, Britain's citizens were treated to the unedifying spectacle of limbless veterans reduced to begging on the streets, their medals for bravery worn across the front of tattered coats.

Another adjustment the returning soldiers had to make was social. During their time away, women had stepped up in their millions to work in war industries, finding financial and psychological independence while their husbands and boyfriends were away. Not surprisingly, many women were reluctant to go back to traditional female roles after the war, and were often rather alienated from the men who returned, very different from the men who had left. Thus the UK divorce rate in 1948 was more than double what it had been in 1938. Similarly in the United States, the divorce rate was 20 per cent in 1940, but 43 per cent in 1946.

Another problem for veterans back in the civilian world was coping with what they had been through. By the end of the First World War, British medical services had treated 80,000 cases of 'shell shock', resulting in what we now call combat stress and post-traumatic stress disorder (PTSD). These were only the most visible cases – tens of thousands of other cases were likely to have gone undiagnosed and untreated. The symptoms of this condition vary, from periodic nightmares and anxiety through to complete physical breakdown and suicidal and violent acts (such as domestic violence). The triggers are also equally varied. For some soldiers, a single horrifying incident can embed itself in the memory and only emerge, like some forgotten ghost, in later life. For other soldiers, the repeated daily grind of combat and its associated stress produce a complete and prolonged mental burnout. The psychology of PTSD was little understood after both world wars, meaning that millions of men went through the rest of their lives in torment and confusion, little understood by the society into which they were trying to reintegrate. All sides were affected by the phenomenon. Amongst German troops, for example, there were reports of up to 33 per cent of all military hospitalisations being psychological by 1944–45.

US VETERANS STATISTICS
– IRAQ AND AFGHANISTAN

Number of
US veterans
2.3 million

Percentage
suffering from
post-traumatic
stress disorder
(PTSD)
14–20 per cent

Estimated
percentage of
veterans with
traumatic brain
injury (TBI)
19 per cent

Percentage of
veterans suffering
problems with
alcohol abuse
39 per cent

Percentage of
veterans with
PTSD and TBI
7 per cent

Today we have far better understanding of veterans' needs, experiences and problems, but we must not be complacent. Amongst veterans of the Afghanistan and Iraq conflicts, rates of suicide and violence remain worryingly high in men plagued by PTSD. For example, in the United States the US Department of Veteran Affairs estimates that PTSD afflicts:

- Almost 31 per cent of Vietnam veterans
- As many as 10 per cent of Gulf War (*Desert Storm*) veterans
- 11 per cent of veterans of the war in Afghanistan
- 20 per cent of Iraqi war veterans

The rates in British veterans of Afghanistan and Iraq do not appear to be quite as high, but there are still issues to be addressed. For example, a *Sunday Mirror* report in 2013 revealed that an estimated 9,000 military veterans were homeless on Britain's streets, the ex-soldiers making up 10 per cent of the homeless total. Furthermore, in 2012 forty-four British soldiers were killed in Afghanistan, but fifty serving soldiers or veterans took their own lives in the same year.

Another challenge of modern war is helping soldiers who have been injured get back into work and family life. Across the coalition forces, thousands of men and women have suffered limb amputations, head trauma or other debilitating injuries. We should never underestimate the challenges facing such people. In many cases, particularly those involving limb amputations, the wounded soldier has to adjust to an entirely new type of existence, in which simple and once-familiar physical tasks become alien and exhausting. Studies in the United States have shown that 25 per cent of combat amputees typically suffer from PTSD, and more than 35 per cent from chronic depression. Thus while mobility can usually be restored by intelligent aftercare and the application of excellent prosthetics, providing the support to get wounded soldiers back into work and society at large is expensive, time-consuming and utterly justified.

Of course, it is not just military personnel who experience the consequences of war. For every soldier deployed, their families must also adjust to the mental hardships of not seeing a son, daughter, spouse or parent for months on end, and worrying about their exposure to danger. The families have to cope with the practical demands of separation, frequently involving money worries and the need to take over responsibilities previously performed by their partners. If a soldier returns home injured, then the family must also reconfigure their lives. If a soldier is killed, the family has to cope with both the tremendous and enduring shock of grief, together with their worries for the future.

RESPONDING TO NEED

As we have seen, the military community has its vulnerabilities, as well as its multitude of strengths. Yet if we look across Britain, and across history, we find plenty of encouraging examples of men, women and children who devote their time, money and energy to helping this vital sector of society. During and after the First World War, charities for military servicemen proliferated. For example, in 1915 Sir Cyril Arthur Pearson, a newspaper and publishing magnate, established a hostel for blinded soldiers in Bayswater Hill, London. (Pearson had special sympathies with the blind, having lost his sight to glaucoma in the early 1900s.) The hostel focused upon the men's rehabilitation into the workforce, building up their physical strength and emotional resilience. In 1923 this charity was known as the St Dunstan's Home, and it survives to this day in the form of Blind Veterans UK.

The issue of rehabilitating the huge numbers of paraplegics was further embraced by the charitable sector. 'Curative workshops' appeared, in which volunteers assisted wounded soldiers in regaining their physical fitness (using specially adapted gym equipment). Other groups took a different approach.

The Chailey and Agnes Hunt's Orthopedic Hospital, for example, specialized in the care of disabled children. During the war, however, it also began to look after crippled soldiers. One interesting element of its work was to pair the wounded soldier with a child, and make the soldier act as an inspiration and help to the young person.

Also in 1915, the Star & Garter Committee was established under the auspices of the British Red Cross. The focus of the Committee was the support and rehabilitation of severely disabled veterans, and the purchase of the Star & Garter Hotel on Richmond Hill gave the organisation its first premises as well as inspiring its name. Some sixty-five wounded veterans were admitted in 1916 (the average age was 22), and the charity's volunteers either helped them back into their previous lives or provided a meaningful existence within the home. As with the St Dunstan's Home, these early efforts were just the start of a long history of support, and today the Royal Star & Garter Homes deliver nursing and medical care to ex-service personnel. Not all work with disabled veterans was performed by the voluntary sector. In 1919 the government put in place the King's National Roll Scheme (KNRS), a voluntary scheme that encouraged companies with more than ten employees to employ at least 5 per cent of their workforce from disabled servicemen.

The scheme was a success, employing 89,000 people in its first year and running until 1944 (when the Disabled Persons' Employment Act was brought in).

As we have seen, the motivation to help ex-servicemen and women flowered strongly in the First World War, and has continued to this day. The Royal British Legion is a case in point. The vast fundraising efforts of The Royal British Legion are focused on supporting millions of veterans and serving members of the armed forces, plus their families. The forms that this help can take are as varied as the lives of the military community. For families suffering bereavement, The Royal British Legion provides advice on dealing with the legal complexities of inquiries and inquests, or financial support if required. Its services for veterans include help with setting up a business (through the 'Be the Boss' schemes), grants and loans, advice about compensation claims, or assistance with suitable care-home facilities for older veterans.

Some of the most important support work, however, continues to focus on the treatment and rehabilitation of wounded soldiers. For those soldiers suffering from serious wounds, the road to recovery is a long one, requiring a patient human network to help at every stage of progression. The British Ministry of Defence leads the Defence Recovery

BRITISH TROOPS ADMITTED TO FIELD HOSPITAL, 2006–2013

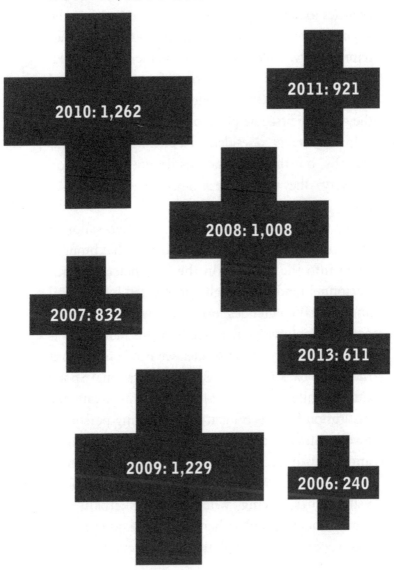

2010: 1,262

2011: 921

2008: 1,008

2007: 832

2013: 611

2009: 1,229

2006: 240

Capability, which works in partnership with The Royal British Legion, Help for Heroes and other charities and agencies to help wounded military personnel gain the support they need to regain independence and either return to service life or enter work in the civilian world. Many of the veterans go to one of several Personnel Recovery Centres (PRCs) dotted around the UK, where they acquire first-rate physical, mental and vocational help. On average, a resident of a PRC will stay for four months, but the organisations do not set limits on recovery – they will devote as much time as it takes.

A key to aiding the recovery of a soldier, sailor or airman is often to tap into the qualities that brought them into the military in the first place. Service personnel tend to be highly motivated by physical and mental challenges, especially with a degree of competition involved. To see how this motivation is applied to wounded personnel, we need only look at the Battle Back Centre, based at the National Sports Centre, Lilleshall, West Midlands. This invaluable institution focuses on getting recovering personnel involved in a variety of sports, in the process confronting and often overcoming the feared limitations of their injuries. Sporting activities include climbing, watersports, caving, wheelchair basketball, clay pigeon shooting and archery, and some 600 veterans pass successfully through the centre every year.

DECLINE IN US SECOND WORLD WAR VETERANS, 2000–16

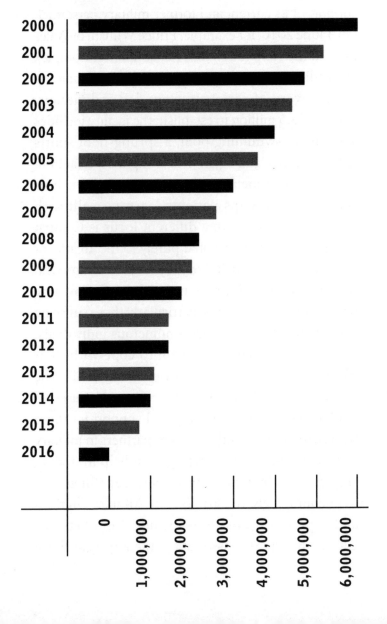

Looking across the UK, we find repeated examples of organisations and individuals investing in the support of its current and former military personnel. On 4 June 2010, for example, Prince William of Wales opened the Help for Heroes Rehabilitation Complex at Headley Court, a state-of-the-art facility for aiding the recovery of seriously wounded individuals. Costing £8.5 million to establish, the facility includes a 25-metre swimming pool, a sprung-floor sports hall, a cardiovascular gym with anti-gravity treadmill, numerous treatment rooms and also a gait analysis centre, which helps patients learn to walk with prosthetic limbs. With a different focus is Combat Stress UK, a charity devoted purely to the 'treatment and support of British Armed Forces Veterans who have mental health problems'. Through providing free treatment to veterans, particularly those suffering from PTSD, the charity helps numerous individuals, old and young, enabling them to cope with their psychological wounds and move forward in life. The Army Widows' Association, by contrast, focuses its work on providing friendship and support for those who have lost husbands, wives or partners in military service, the assistance ranging from help in finding employment through to one-to-one counselling.

Encouragingly, the list goes on. Military charities and support organisations include Blind Veterans UK, the Burma Star Association, the Royal Air Force

AMPUTEES FROM LANDMINES, PER 10,000 INHABITANTS

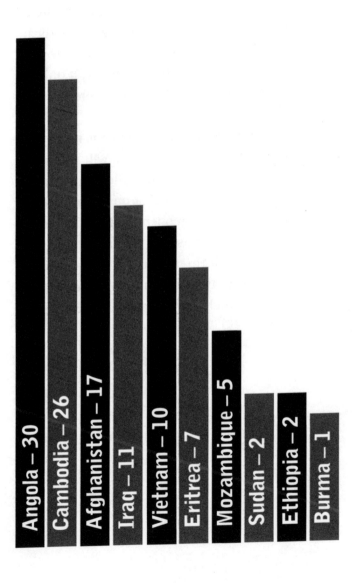

Benevolent Fund, Royal Navy and Royal Marines Charity, Veteran's Aid and the Forces Pension Society. Taken together, such organisations signal that thousands of people care enough to dedicate themselves to the welfare of serving and former military personnel. It is important work, if only for the reason that it sends a message of appreciation to the armed forces.

This is not a jingoistic statement. It is made with the full awareness that not everyone will agree with the conflicts in which soldiers, sailors and airmen serve. Yet the point remains that on a human level, soldiers are compelled, frequently on our behalf, to go out and face situations that are dangerous in the extreme, and which threaten their very existence. It is on account of their humanity, not necessarily the causes for which they fight, that they deserve our support.

CONCLUSION

NOT EVERYONE AGREES with the sentiments behind the poppy. In recent years, several high-profile individuals have levelled various charges against poppy wearing, with the accusations ranging from the glorification or war through to the trivialising of the dead. Some say that the poppy is a blind act of patriotism, a sentimentalising of violence that actually prevents us from seeing the horror, moral complexity and reality of what actually happens in conflict.

There is, it has to be admitted, a danger in wearing any symbol linked to war. We can never see the motivations of those who buy and wear the Remembrance Poppy. Many will buy one largely without thinking, dropping the coin into the charity box while rushing on to some other appointment. Others, by contrast, might wear the poppy through nationalistic motivations, seeing it as a distinctly British and oppositional act of patriotism. Some may even wear the poppy simply because everyone else is.

We can never, nor should we, control the tapestry of reasons for which people buy the poppy. I would argue, however, that the poppy does have an aggregate positive effect on both society and the individual. For a start, the poppy is not an isolated purchase, but is tied to a distinct period in the national calendar, culminating in the profound two-minute silence on Remembrance Day.

When the nation stops, it is compelled to reflect on war and its consequences, and in that moment the poppy really comes alive in its meaning and power. For the rest of the year, most of our attention is soaked up by the daily realities of work and family. When we buy a poppy, however, we might pause, just for a second, and step out of our own narrative to reflect on the magnitude of war. Once we do that, we raise the chances of being more engaged with the realities of war, not more distant from them.

The poppy is also about education. The world wars are becoming ever-more distant in time, and for the younger generations these conflicts are starting to subside into the history books. We have to be honest about this and accept that time does change our relationship to events. The Seven Years' War was doubtless traumatic for millions of people around the world when it occurred, but dozens of generations have been born and died since those days, so the war's impact is no longer felt on an emotional level.

However, the Remembrance Poppy is not just about the First World War, Second World War, the Falklands War, the war in Afghanistan, or indeed any specific conflict. The poppy compels us to address war in general, and ask fundamental questions. Why does it happen? What is it like? Who suffers? Who helps those who suffer? It also directs our attention to the conflicts that are ongoing – even as I write these words, people continue to fight and die, whether on their home soil or in a foreign land.

It is a sad fact that war is a constant visitor to our planet. The poppy will always, therefore, be relevant. What it says is that by not forgetting those who have died in the past, there are seeds of hope for the future.

APPENDIX

BOOKS

Arthur, Max, *Forgotten Voices of the Great War: A New History of WWI in the Words of the Men and Women Who Were There* (London; Ebury Press, 2003)

Frank, Anne, *The Diary of Anne Frank* (London; Doubleday Books, 2003)

Hastings, Max, *All Hell Let Loose: The World at War 1939–1945* (London; Harper Press, 2012)

Hennesey, Patrick, *The Junior Officers' Reading Club: Killing Time and Fighting Wars* (London; Penguin 2010)

Holmes, Richard (ed.), *The Oxford Companion to Military History* (Oxford; OUP, 2001)

Holmes, Richard, *Tommy: The British Soldier on the Western Front 1914–18* (London; Harper Collins, 2004)

Keegan, John, *The Face of Battle: A Study of Agincourt, Waterloo and the Somme* (London; Pimlico, 2004)

MacDonald, Lyn *Passchendaele: The Story of the Third Battle of Ypres 1917* (London; Penguin, 1993)

Price, Sian, *If You Are Reading This ...: Last Letters from the Front Line* (Barnsley; Frontline Books, 2011)

Sajer, Guy, *The Forgotten Soldier* (London; Cassell Military, 1999)

Saunders, Nicholas J., *The Poppy: A Cultural History from Ancient Egypt to Flanders Fields to Afghanistan* (London; Oneworld publications, 2013)

Stallworthy, Jon, *The Oxford Book of War Poetry* (Oxford; OUP, 2008)

Willmot, H.P. *World War I* (London; Dorling Kindersely, 2009)

VETERAN SUPPORT ORGANISATIONS

Army Benevolent Fund – www.soldierscharity.org

Army Widows Association – www.armywidows.org.uk

Combat Stress – www.combatstress.org.uk

Help for Heroes – www.helpforheroes.org.uk

Royal Air Force Benevolent Fund – www.rafbf.org

Royal Navy and Royal Marines Charity – rnrmc.org.uk

Soldiers, Sailors, Airmen and Families Association (SSAFA) – www.ssafa.org.uk

The Royal British Legion – www.britishlegion.org.uk

MAJOR UK MUSEUMS

Bletchley Park – www.bletchleypark.org.uk
Cardiff Castle Museum of the Welsh Soldier –
    www.cardiffcastlemuseum.org.uk
Eden Camp – www.edencamp.co.uk
Edinburgh Castle/National War Museum –
    www.edinburghcastle.gov.uk
Fleet Air Arm Museum – www.fleetairarm.com
Imperial War Museum – www.iwm.org.uk
Royal Air Force Museum – rafmuseum.org.uk
Royal Naval Museum – www.royalnavalmuseum.org
The Tank Museum – www.tankmuseum.org

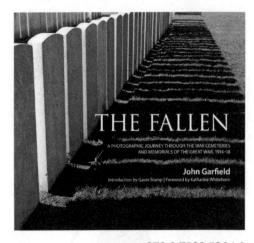

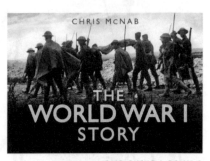